PUB WALKS
IN SOUTH SURREY

Forty Circular Walks

WELCOME TO
THE MILL AT ELSTEAD

D1392696

Around South Surrey Inns

John Quarendon

Other publications in the series
"Pub Walks in Dorset"
"Forty More Pub Walks in Dorset"
"Pub Walks in Somerset "
"Pub Walks in West Sussex"
"Pub Walks in East Sussex"
"Pub Walks in Kent"
"Pub Walks in Hants & the IOW"
"Pub Walks in Devon"
"Pub Walks in Cornwall"
"Pub Walks in the New Forest"
"Pub Walks in Hardy's Wessex"
"Mike Power's Pub Walks Along the Dorset Coast"
"Pub Walks in North Surrey"

1st edition published April 2003

Acknowledgements
Thanks once again to my wife Margaret, who trod every mile and proof read and to my daughter Suzy, who typed up all my notes.

© John Quarendon

ISBN 1898073252

Power Publications
1 Clayford Ave
Ferndown, Dorset.
BH22 9PQ
sales@powerpublications.co.uk

Publishers note:
Whilst every care has been taken to ensure that all the information contained in this book is correct neither the author nor the publisher can accept any responsibility for any inaccuracies that might occur.

Printed by Pardy & Son (Printers) Ltd, Ringwood, Hants.
Front cover: The Mill at Elstead
Layout: Mike Power.
Photographs and drawings: John Quarendon.

Introduction

The task with 'Forty Walks in N. Surrey' (still available if you hurry!) was to find attractive walks in an increasingly built up area. In the 'Beautiful South' traversed by several long distance trails, the task was to find hitherto unpublished walks. Many villages now only have one pub and describing a circle of approximately 4 miles around them, avoiding road walking, presents few options. The result may not be all new ground but if any seem familiar I hope that is because they are revisiting favourite places.

The Walks

The Walks are circular between 3½ and 5½ miles and designed to start and finish at the featured pub. Twenty of the walks intersect with others to give the option of longer rambles of 7-10 miles. Alternative free parking facilities en route are indicated on the maps with the letter P and nearby railway stations are also indicated. The maps are generally in proportion but not precisely to scale.

You can usually get away with summer walking in trainers but on Surrey's heavy soils I strongly recommend walking boots at other times or where the walk description warns of mud. Footpaths are often poorly maintained and long trousers offer protection against nettles, brambles and insects. A walking stick is a useful aid on overgrown paths and, when raised, seems to act as a deterrent to over inquisitive heifers. An Ordnance Survey, Explorer Series, 1:25000 map, a compass, Swiss army knife, antihistamine bite/sting treatment, compact binoculars and compact camera are useful walking companions and should all fit into a decent sized bum bag.

The format of the Forty Walks series is designed to give maximum value for money in terms of the number of walks. It does not allow space for much background information so the main landmarks and places of historical interest are only referred to in passing. For the same reason the bird watching notes are restricted to the more unusual sightings.

The Pubs

In those cases where a choice of pubs was available on the planned route the selection criteria were choice of real ales and wines; appetising original menus with snacks and main meals, stressing the use of fresh ingredients and home cooking; value for money; low volume of any music and separation of amusements from the dining area. Ambience is important and the sort of welcome you get when you approach the bar. As I know to my cost it is sensible to check if the pub is still open before travelling and also to book in advance for parties, particularly on Sundays. Please ask permission before parking to walk. Pubs are constantly changing hands, changing character or being closed down. If what you find here is not what you find there, you will know that another one has bitten the dust in the interval between the writing and the walking.

The Country Code

Please keep to footpaths, shut all gates, damage no property, light no fires, dig no bulbs, leave no litter and keep dogs on leads near livestock. Kiss at all kissing gates if suitably accompanied. If not hang about for the U3A party coming along behind. Somebody's granny/grandad might make your day.

South Surrey
Map of Walk Locations

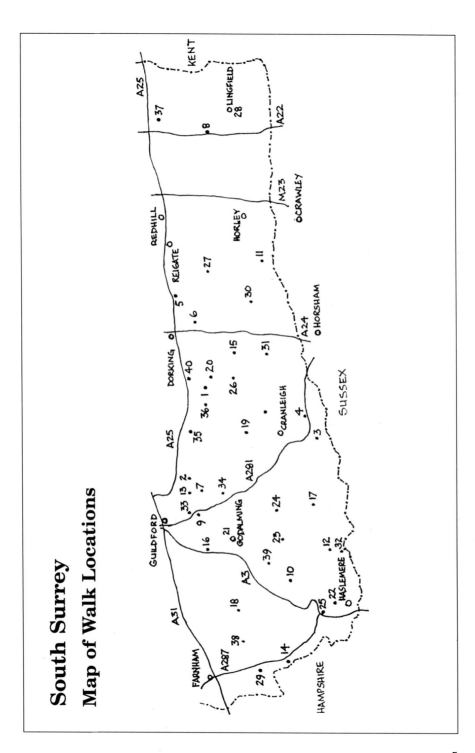

The Abinger Hatch, Abinger Common

The Abinger Hatch is hidden away down a narrow lane in an idyllic spot opposite the duck pond and church. I need more space than I have here to extol its virtues so I must resort to a list.

There are five real ales, including Tanglefoot, London Pride, Young's Special and their own Abinger Hatch, brewed by Weltons and 4 wines by the glass.

The menu, covering several blackboards, is extraordinarily comprehensive including nine salads, nine ploughman's, seven vegetarian dishes such as vegetable Kiev and quorn sausages, nachos, steaks, deep fried catch of the day, chicken Madras and on and on. There are even take away curries, fish and chips and sausages. The children's menu offers a choice of 7 dishes. All this in a comfortable welcoming local with a nice garden and a separate restaurant.

The ducks come from the pond to beg for food in the garden and dogs are welcome.

Opening hours are Mon-Fri 11.30am-3pm and 5-11pm, weekends open all day. Tel : 01306 730737.

The Abinger Hatch is situated in Abinger Lane opposite the church at Abinger Common. Turn south down Raikes Lane from the A25 between Abinger Hammer and Wotton and take the first turning on the left. There is parking at the pub and opposite.

Approx. distance of walk: 4 miles. Start at OS Map Ref. TQ 116460.

This is a 3 village and 3 pub walk allowing combination with Walks 26 and/or 36. It starts over farmland where skylarks sing and then through woodland with one steep hill.

1. Go forward from the pub through the church gate and out the other side onto a gravel path. Enjoy the views and the skylarks as you cross fields via cattle grids and then go between hedges to Raikes Farm. Turn R between houses into the farmyard then L at a waymark on a barn out to Raikes Lane. Turn L and bear R past The Volunteer pub (Walk 36) and at a 'T' junction turn R. In 60 yards turn L up steps onto a fenced path. At a lane turn L and in 25 yards R past a metal barrier. Keep beside the fence on the R and at a lane turn L. At a junction go ahead for 10 yards then turn R on a footpath. Maintain direction over tarmac, then path again, over a stile and between fields. At a waymark post turn L along the margin of a field and a bluebell wood. Cross a stile and continue on a path past a fingerpost and then a stile and gate on

the L. At a fork go L and at a waymark post turn L on a wide track.

2. Pass the Holmbury Youth Hostel car park on your L (in 2002 there was some talk of the Hostel closing) and continue in woods. Bear half R over a crossing track and down hill. Go over a wide crossing track and uphill. Pass a turning on the R and at a fork go L down to a road at Holmbury St Mary.

3. To your right is the Royal Oak (Walk 26) but you turn L. After ½ mile turn R on a signed bridleway, over a crossing track and steeply uphill. (If this is slippery after rain see alternative path (dotted arrows on map). Go over a crossing path and at a fork go L uphill. Continue over a crossing path at the bottom of a slope then bear L with a fence on the L. At a road turn L through Abinger Common village and back to the pub.

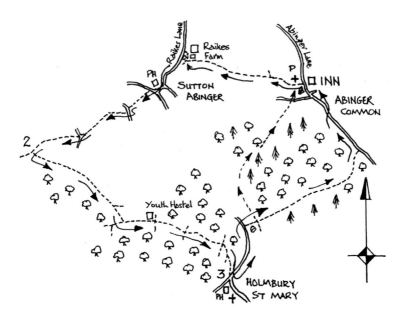

The Drummond Arms, Albury

A hotel with letting rooms, including one with a four-poster bed, The Drummond Arms has an up market ambience with a sunny conservatory and a pleasant garden.

The bar is cosy enough with Old Speckled Hen, Gales HSB, Brakspears and Courage Best on offer.

The extensive menu has a good range of baguettes, jackets, burgers and vegetarian dishes and a more expensive range of "butcher's" and "fisherman's" specialities. Blackboard specials included sausages and mash and home made moussaka. Children can have small portions of some adult meals.

Dogs in the garden only please. Lunch is served from 12-2pm daily and evening opening is 6-11pm.

Tel : 01483 202039.

The Drummond Arms is situated in Albury Street, the A248 turning south off the A25 between Guildford and Dorking. There is ample parking at the pub. The walk passes within 500 yards of Chilworth Railway Station.

Approx. distance of walk: 5 miles. Start at OS Map Ref. TQ 050479. The walk may be combined with Walk 13 at Point 3 and Walk 7 at Point 4.

This favourite walk rises to the Pilgrims' Way before descending through a bluebell wood to pretty ponds along the R. Tillingbourne. It continues over farmland past more ponds and masses of orchids in June, before exploring the plantations of the Albury Estate.

1. Turn R out of the pub and R again up Water Lane. Pass a farm and ignore a way-mark post on the L. Just before a signed bridleway on the R turn up L on an unsigned path. This is the Pilgrims' Way. Go through a gate and across a field, then another gate and over a crossing track. Llamas in the field on the L flushed a noisy partridge that in turn caused two young tawny owls to make a brief appearance on the R. A rare treat.

2. Cross Guildford Lane diagonally R and continue into woods. At a 'T' junction before a car park, turn L and immediately fork L. Go over a crossing track by a waymark post and downhill. At a 'T' junction turn R through bluebells in season and L at the next 'T' junction. The path rises through Colyer's Hanger then descends to a road by Millstream Cottage. Turn sharp L here on an unsigned path with a pond to your R. Cross a stile into a garden and con-

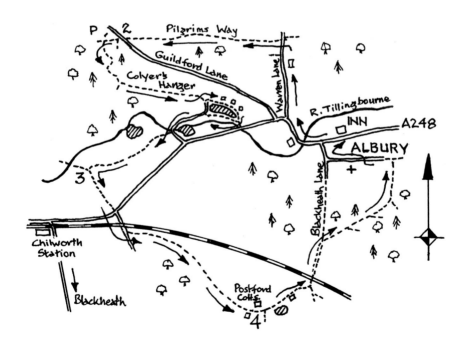

Walk No. 2

tinue between houses and the pond. Just before the A248 turn R on a path between the R Tillingbourne and the pond. At the end of the pond maintain direction on the road still beside the river. Pass another pond and bear L over the pond outlet then bear half R on a signed footpath. Maintain direction over 3 stiles and 3 meadows passing another pond to your R. A final stile leads to a track where turn sharp L. (Turning R here would lead in a few yards to Point 4 of Walk 13 should you wish to combine the two.)

3. Continue on the track to reach the A248. Chilworth Railway Station is 500 yds to the right. Cross into Dorking Road and over a railway bridge. Turn L through a metal gate and bear half L beside a wooden fence to a gate. Cross a field with views of the Downs and Albury Church, then go over 2 stiles to enter the Albury Estate. A grass path

between fields leads to a track past Postford Farm Cottages (Point 2 on Walk 7).

4. Bear L over a stream and past another pond. In June look out for masses of orchids in the marshy ground around the pond as you progress up the lane. Just before a 'T' junction fork up L on a footpath, over a stile and along the edge of a field. Go through a kissing gate and cross the railway.

5. Go through another kissing gate and along a field edge to descend to Blackheath Lane. (Turn L for a short cut back to the pub – see map.) Otherwise cross over to a wide track uphill. Pass a gate and at a fork go L. At a waymark post turn L on a sunken path downhill. Ignore side paths and look out for weasels hunting rabbits as this is Warren Lane. At a 'T' junction turn L. The path narrows to meet Church Lane. Pass the church and the road bends R back to the A248, where turn R back to the pub.

Waterloo Pond

The Crown, Alfold

The Crown had been run more as a hobby than a business for some years before new tenants in November 2002 spruced it up and revamped the menu. There is a cosy bar and separate dining area with an open fire in winter. Outside is a small patio and a grassy garden.

It is a Green King house offering their popular Abbot Ale and IPA alongside Old Speckled Hen or Ruddles County and a Green King extra such as Triumph or 1799.

The printed menu offers a choice of snacks – sandwiches plain and toasted, ploughman's, jackets and baguettes plus staple main courses such as jumbo battered cod, breaded scampi, gammon steak, vegetarian schnitzel etc. The specials board features homemade pies, lasagne, grilled trout, vegetarian and local organic meat dishes.

Children and dogs are welcome.

Opening times are Monday-Saturday 11am-3pm and 5-11pm, Sunday 12 noon-4pm and 7-10.30pm.

Tel: 01403 752216.

Walk No. 3

The Crown is situated in the centre of Alfold on the B2133 about 4 miles south of Cranleigh. There is a car park behind the pub.

Approx. distance of walk: 4 miles. Start at OS Map Ref. TQ 038340.

A flattish walk mostly on farmland with a section beside the disused Wey and Arun Canal and another through a bluebell wood. The route passes five ponds with much bird life.

1. Turn R out of the pub up the path to St Nicholas' Church, passing the remains of the stocks on the L. Bear R past the porch to a road, where turn L then L again into the cemetery. Ignore the path and keep to the LH hedge to exit via a kissing gate. Maintain direction down a field and over a stile. Bear half R across a field, over a stile and up the next field beside the fence. Cross a stile to the tarmac drive to Turtles Farm. Turn R then in a few yards sharp L to follow the drive up past a pretty pond, where a heron was sampling the goldfish. Just before the drive turns L between ponds turn R across grass to a gate. Bear half L across the field to a metal gate and follow the fingerpost to another gate. Follow the footpath forward then L along the edge of a field to cross the stile in the corner. Maintain direction across the middle of a field and over a stile. Go forward through a gate and between ponds. At an amputee fingerpost turn L with the pond on your L. At the next fingerpost turn R across a field to a gate.

(this may be hidden behind a nettle patch in season.)
2. Cross a footbridge and turn R beside the old Wey and Arun canal for half a mile. At Rosemary Lane turn R for about 700 yards. About 80 yards past Furzens Cottage on the R turn L on a waymarked bridleway into woods. This is Sachelhill Lane and you stay on this through bluebell woods for about ½ mile.
3. Pass a house and barns on the L and turn sharp R into the Springbok Estate, passing between houses and a fishpond. Where the drive bends R bear L on a concrete drive. The correct path is over a stile on the R – see dotted arrows on map but to avoid disturbing the cows usually in this field I suggest – go forward on the drive and follow it R past a post box. Go over a stile on the L and head up the field about 10 yards to the R of a telegraph pole to another stile beyond. Keep to the R edge of a meadow to cross a stile in a fence onto a path to Rosemary Lane, where turn L back to the pub.

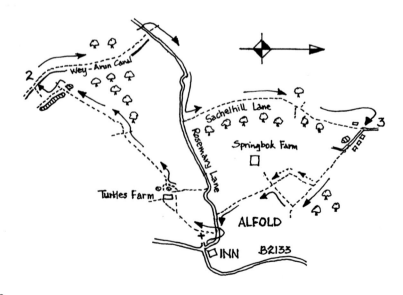

The Thurlow Arms, Baynards

When you order a pint of ale and the landlord says "It is in beautiful condition Sir, I've just tried it myself", you know that you are in a proper pub. Mr Gibbs, the gentlemanly landlord and his daughter, a talented cook, run the sort of pub you can only wish was at the end of your own street. The décor is eccentric. The walls and ceiling are covered in hundreds of artefacts and memorabilia from a fireman's helmet to an armadillo skin handbag. There is a pool table and dartboard.

They have Ringwood Forty-Niner and Best, Hogs Back TEA and Badger Best.

Burgers, sandwiches, jackets and ploughmans are supplemented by home made steak and ale pie, beef lasagne and homemade puddings. The ham off the bone was succulent and the chicken curry was delicious. There is a separate childrens' menu.

Dogs on leads are welcome in the pub and the garden.

Opening hours are Mon-Sat 11am-3pm and 6-11pm. Sunday 12-10.30pm. Last orders for food at lunchtime 2pm.

Tel : 01403 822459.

Walk No. 4

Baynards is signed on two turnings north off the A281 Horsham road about 1 mile west of Rudgwick. The pub is signed at the junction of Baynards Rd and Cox Green Rd. There is parking at the pub.

Approx. distance of walk: 4½ miles. Start at OS Map Ref. TQ 076351.

A walk on the Downs Link and Sussex Border Path through dairy and sheep farms and bluebell woods. Do it in May/June for all the lambs, calves and pheasants and the chance of getting goosed in the woods.

1. Go forward from the pub and turn R on the Downs Link. Pass the former Baynards Station featured in the film Railway Children. Turn L at a fingerpost then R through a gate under an arch and past a barrier. Cross a plank bridge and bear L to another and turn R signed Downs Link. Continue in a bluebell wood past a Surrey/Sussex border marker and down to turn L over a stile into a large meadow. Maintain direction over a stile and a second long field to a stile in the corner then with a fence to your L and through a bluebell wood uphill to a gate. Bear half R across a small field and exit along a field edge, then on an enclosed path. Bear R on a track down to Cox Green Road.

2. Cross to a fingerpost and go ahead through trees to a field where keep close to the RH edge for about 200 yards. At the corner of the fence turn R to a waymarked stile by a gate. At a fingerpost bear L across a field to the corner of a copse, where turn L for 30 yards then R into the copse. Pass a fenced bluebell wood full of pheasants and at a waymark post turn L along a field edge to a road junction. Cross to a finger post and enter woods. We were greeted here by free range chickens, geese, goslings and one extraordinarily handsome turkey all loose in the woods. Pass some pens and a house on the R and keep to the RH side along two fields. In front of Home Farm bear L to a footbridge and look for herons at the pond. Go forward to a stile and out to a lane.

3. Turn L and at a house keep ahead on a track. Pass Collins Farm and Collins Copse, another bluebell wood. Just past a waymarked gate on the R turn L on a wide track across a clearing and L again on the Downs Link back to the pub.

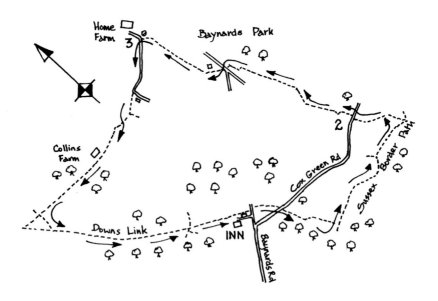

The Red Lion, Betchworth

The Red Lion had never disappointed so it was with some trepidation that we entered past the 'Under New Management' banner in July 2002. Fortunately the character of this comfortable former coaching inn that once brewed its own ale seemed unmolested. Vital evidence came in the four real ales including Old Speckled Hen and Adnams Broadside.

The fresh fish delivery arrived as we did and the blackboard menu included sea bass, salmon, cod, tiger prawns and dressed crab salad plus other interesting items like venison steak, rump of lamb and tortilloni al pesto. Snacks included sandwiches, baguettes, jackets and ploughmans.

Fresh freesias on the tables was a nice touch. The wisteria clad rear entrance and sunny patio and garden are high above the road.

There is a separate annex with 8 en-suite rooms.

Children are welcome but dogs on leads in the garden only.

The pub is open all day every day. Lunch is served from 12-3pm and dinner from 6-9pm.

Tel : 01737 845242.

Walk No. 5

The Red Lion is reached by turning south off the A25 at the roundabout half way between Dorking and Reigate and turning L at the 'T' junction into Old Reigate Road. The walk passes within half a mile of Betchworth Station. There is parking at the pub.

Approx. distance of walk: 5½ miles. Start at OS Map Ref. TQ 214505.

This is a 3 village walk passing 4 pubs, 3 churches and a bluebell wood, crossing the R.Mole twice and returning along the Greensand Way where skylarks sing. There are fine views over the Mole Valley to Box Hill.

1. Leave the back of the pub car park along the LH edge of the cricket field. Maintain direction beside the next field and at a fence corner bear half R to a telegraph pole. Cross the A25 to a fingerpost and follow the edge of a field to a stile. Bear half R across a field to another stile and pass houses to turn R on a lane. Fork R onto a footpath before the much photographed Buckland Pond and recross the A25. Turn R then L into Dungate Lane and fork R before gates. Cross a GW waymarked stile on the R and head across a field towards 2 sheds. Turn R over the stile and along the field edge with Box Hill ahead. Cross a stile and at the bottom of steps turn L then L again into Sandy Lane.

2. At Wonham Lane turn R and at a 'T' junction by the Dolphin pub go forward towards the church gate and turn L on the footpath beside the wall of Betchworth House. Cross the R Mole and turn R over a stile, across a meadow and through woods. At a fork keep R, emerge over a stile and keep beside the fence on the R. When the copse ends maintain direction along a line of oaks to a stile on the corner of a bluebell wood. Continue along the field edge and turn R at the corner of the wood down to a stile. Cross the meadow diagonally L and turn R on a fenced path. Pass allotments and houses to reach a road.

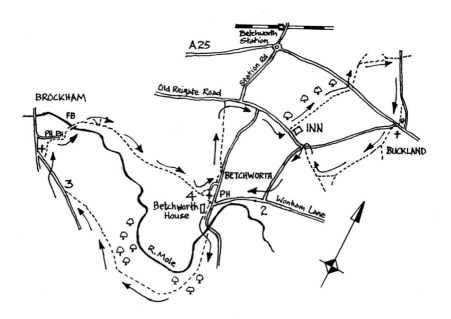

3. Turn R and just before a church bear R past a barrier onto Brockham Green. Bear R towards the Royal Oak and Duke's Head and turn R in front of the latter rejoining the GW. Opposite the old livestock pound turn L through a small gate. Cross a footbridge and bear R on a track above the river. At a fingerpost fork R past gardens. Keep to this path for half a mile and listen out for skylarks.

4. You may wish to visit St Michael's churchyard, used in 'Four Weddings and a Funeral', but for the walk turn L before the gate. Turn L again at a 'T' junction and again past a barrier onto a footpath. Cross a grass area and the end of a road to continue on a footpath with a field on your L. Turn R at the Old Reigate Road and ignoring side turnings return to the pub.

Bluebell Wood, Brockham

The Plough, Blackbrook

Hall and Woodhouse have wisely done nothing to change this deservedly popular pub, which has a central bar dividing the pub into smoking and non smoking rooms. Dogs are only allowed in the former so non-smoking dog owners had best make for the attractive umbrella filled garden. Children are welcome anywhere.

The enhanced range of ales includes Tanglefoot, Champion, Badger and Sussex. There are twelve wines and five ports by the glass and 13 country wines are available.

The snack menu offers seven ploughman's, seven jackets, toasted 'deli' filled baguettes e.g. char grilled vegetables, melted mozzarella and basil pesto and steak sandwiches, etc. The blackboard menu includes curries, moussaka, chilli, steaks and lamb chops with more exotic dishes like paw paw stuffed with crab remoulade and twice cooked plum sautéed pork and rice. Salads can be custom made.

Hours are 11am-2.30pm and 6-11pm Monday to Friday. Saturday 11am-3.30pm and 6-11pm and Sunday 12-3.30pm and 7-10.30pm.

Tel : 01306 886603.

Walk No. 6

From the A24 south from Dorking fork L into Blackbrook Lane after 1 mile. The Plough is 1 mile on the left hand side. There is parking at the pub.

Approx. distance of walk: 3½ miles. Start at OS Map Ref. TQ 181467.

A walk in search of the elusive roe deer in the wilds of Holmwood Common, with a brief excursion to Redlands Wood, curtailed by path closures. Paths on the common are usually muddy.

1. From the pub cross the road to a footpath into woodland. Skylarks sing over the fields to the R. Stay on this path ignoring side paths to cross a footbridge, then a raised crossing path and another footbridge. Join a road to reach the dual carriageway A24.
2. Cross into Norfolk Lane, turn L at a fingerpost and bear R past No.15 to a stile. Continue up a long meadow to a stile in the top RH corner. Enter Redlands Wood and soon reach a path coming in from the left. The path ahead to Coldharbour was closed by Forestry authorities in July 2002 but while looking in vain for an alternative route we disturbed 2 adult roe deer, so mission accomplished anyway. Turn sharp left and follow the path as it swings round the boundary of the field you crossed earlier and back to the stile. Turn R then R again on the drive to Woodend. Pass houses and

recross the A24 to a waymarked grassy bridleway. Go over a crossing track to reach a large clearing with fine views.
3. Maintain direction following the yellow waymark arrow. Go over 2 waymarked crossing paths and at the next yellow waymark turn L on a narrow path. Cross two sleeper bridges and a crossing path. Ignore 2 narrow paths to the R then fork R to a wide grass track. Two more roe deer ran away from us here. Turn R and stay on this track past waymarked side paths. At a fork keep L on the grass track. About 100 yards before Blackbrook Road turn L on a narrow crossing path. Keep R at 2 forks, then downhill. At a clearing go ahead passing a blue waymark post on your L into a tunnel through holly bushes. Bear L then R at a fork and at a 'T' junction turn R back to the pub.

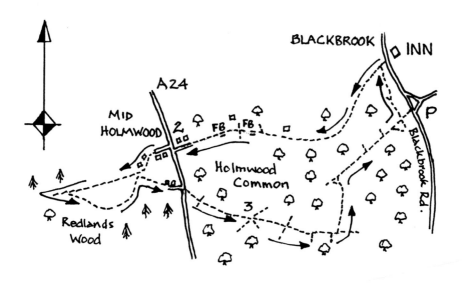

19

The Villagers, Blackheath

Fortunately the Villagers provides an exception to the general rule that chain owned pubs are fit only for the accountants who have destroyed their character. Owned by Leisure Alternatives and run by charming staff this pub is hard to fault.

Four real ales include Hogs Back TEA and their own Blackheath, brewed by Morrells and there are 6 wines by the glass.

As well as the usual run of bar meals the extensive blackboard menu has an international flavour e.g. lamb rogan josh, Mexican chicken, spicy vegetable curry, Thai fish cakes, pasta bake, as well as several fresh fish dishes daily. Children are catered for with a 2 course choice for £2.99 (2002) and a well equipped play area in the garden.

Dogs are welcome in the public bar, patio and garden. Also in the garden is an apple tree with mistletoe growing at shoulder level.

The pub is open all day every day with lunch from 12-2.30pm, 12-4pm Sunday and dinner 6-9.30pm, 7-9pm Sunday. Letting rooms are available.

Tel : 01483 893152.

To reach The Villagers from the A25 turn south on the A248, Albury Street, then south again at Chilworth station. After ½ mile turn L at Blackheath crossroads. There is parking at the pub or in a public car park a little further on.

Approx. distance of walk: 4½ miles. Start at OS Map Ref. TQ 034463.

This walk may be combined with Walk 2 at Point 2 or at Chilworth – see map – with Walk 13. A favourite walk mainly on sandy heathland paths where route finding requires some concentration. The route also includes a farm section with much bird and wildflower interest and passes some stunning property.

1. Turn L out of the pub and follow the road as it bends L before a car park. Just before houses turn R on a bridleway. Fork L at a blue topped post and at the next fork go L then R on a lower parallel path beside a fence. Turn L round the fence corner and downhill. At the next fence corner keep ahead into woods. The path bends R and at a fork where you can see a field over to the L go R uphill. Ignore faint side paths and at a 'T' junction with a wider path go L downhill. Keep ahead past an Albury Estate notice to reach Postford Farm Cottages. (Point 4 on Walk 2.)

2. This section is common to Walk 2. Turn R along a track, cross a bridge and pass a pond and house. Look out for marsh orchids in June and bulrushes and many wild flowers in July. At a 'T' junction turn sharp R away from Walk 2.

3. In a few yards turn L over a waymarked stile and cross a pleasant meadow with a stream and fishponds below. In July a kestrel watched our approach from the telephone wire, linnets and goldfinches fed on the thistles and a heron was fishing under the inadequate protective netting. Cross a stile and turn L then R through Little Ford

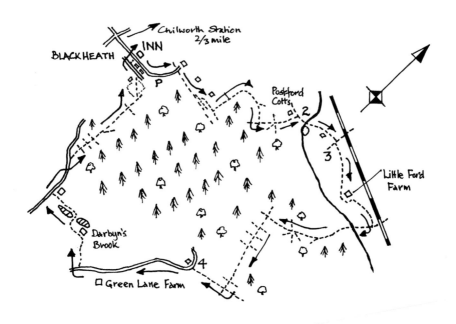

Darbyn's Brook

farmyard. In 80 yards look back for the postcard photograph and at a 'T' junction turn R on a bridleway uphill. At a fork keep R (there is a higher footpath if it is muddy). At a major path junction take the second wide track from the R and in 100 yards turn L on a crossing track. Go over 3 waymarked crossing paths the second with a post numbered 230/232. Pass a clearing with 2 lone pines and head downhill. Go over a crossing path and turn R on a wide crossing path under power lines to reach a road, Green Lane.

4. Turn L for ½ mile passing the magnificent Green Lane Farmhouse and opposite the Green Lane Estate entrance turn R on a path between 2 gates. At the end bear L onto the drive of Darbyn's Brook. Follow the laurel hedge round to the R and sneak a peek R from the bridge at the lovely pond that in June 2002 sported black swans with cygnets. At the road turn R. Where power lines cross the road turn R on a narrow unsigned path uphill. Maintain direction due north over 3 crossing paths and at a fork with 2 blue topped posts keep L ahead. Continue uphill over a crossing path and past a seat and bear L when you can see the cricket pitch. Cross diagonally to the R of the pavilion to a road. Turn L and look for a fenced path between houses on the R that leads back to the pub.

Littleford Farm

The Blue Anchor, Blindley Heath

An inn since the 18th century the Blue Anchor has a spacious interior nicely laid out and refurbished in the old country pub look. It is well done with exposed beams, flagstones and quarry tiles on the floors and 2 open fires.

It is now owned by Vintage Inns and offers that group's standard fare. Bass or Tetley's bitter, a good choice of wines by the glass, the VI menu and good attentive service.

Examples from the menu – see also Walks 33 and 40 – are smoked salmon in tortilla wrap, melon and Parma ham, roasted vegetables and goat's cheese lasagne, chicken Caesar Salad and three shires sausages and mash.

Children are welcome and dogs in the garden only. The garden is at the front and suffers slightly from the proximity of the busy A22. As the sun was shining we sat there anyway and imagined the scene 200 years ago when the only noise would have come from horses hooves and the ale would have been the landlord's own brew.

The pub is open from 12 noon to 11pm daily (10.30pm Sunday) and food is served all day.

Tel : 01342 830001.

Walk No. 8

The Blue Anchor is on the A22 at Blindley Heath, about 4½ miles south of Junction 6 on the M25. There is ample parking at the pub.

Approx. distance of walk: 4½ miles. Start at OS Map Ref. TQ 364455.

A quiet stroll over flat arable farmland with nice views in places.

1. Turn R out of the pub and immediately R at a fingerpost beside the car park. At a fork keep R between hedges. Cross a stile and a field and another stile to an enclosed path. Emerge past a pond onto a drive and at Tandridge Lane turn R then L on the drive to Ardenrun Farm. Continue for ½ mile past Moat Farm. The drive bends L and just before The Barn turn R on a waymarked track. After 350 yards cross a stile on the L and keep to the LH side of a field. At a waymarked gateway bear half R across the field to a waymark post then turn R along the field edge. Maintain direction along the next field with nice views to the R. Turn L through a kissing gate then R, now with the fence on your R.

2. The path bends L along the edge of a copse. Follow the waymarks over a grass crossing path and ignore 2 stiles to the R. Cross the gravel drive to the 15th century Crowhurst Place, sadly out of proper eye-shot, and continue along a field edge. Cross a strip plantation and a footbridge and bear half L across a field. Crowhurst Church is visible on the R and there are views of the North Downs. Approaching the field corner turn R, then immediately L on a farm track. Enter Kingswood Farm yard and fork L past Unit 4. Go through 2 waymarked gates and bear R down the drive of Stocks Farm to turn L on a lane.

3. After 20 yards turn L to a stile, then a waymarked gate and bear half L across a field. Cross 2 stiles and turn L along a field edge. Maintain direction over a stile and another long field. Turn L on Tandridge Lane then R at the drive to Comforts Place Farm. Keep ahead on the grass track for ½ mile. At a 4 way fingerpost turn L. Go beside a metal gate and join a wooded footpath between fields. The path becomes a track, then a lane and at the A22 turn L back to the pub.

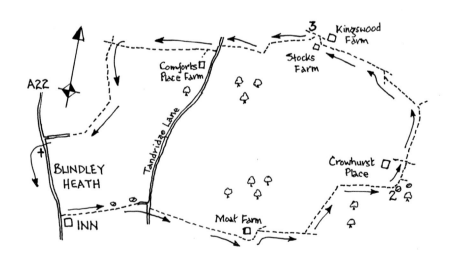

The Parrot Inn, Broadford

The Parrot Inn dates from the 1860's when it was built next to a gunpowder factory. Given the local history of mishaps, it is perhaps fortunate to have survived in its present immaculate state. The pub is welcoming and comfortable, the garden a delight and the lunchtime office 'suits' are contained in the restaurant, where the coffee percolator bubbles constantly.

The ales are Charles Wells' Bombardier, Abbot and London Pride and there is a choice of wines by the glass.

The menu is extensive and there are weekly specials e.g. crab thermidor, veal cordon bleu, oven baked duck breast in orange and cinnamon sauce and home-made burgers, lasagne and vegetarian lasagne.

Well behaved children and dogs on leads are welcome.

There are en-suite letting rooms.

Opening hours are Mon-Sat 11am-3pm and 5.30-11pm. Sunday 12-3pm and 6-10.30pm.

Tel : 01483 456600.

Walk No. 9

The Parrot Inn is situated on the A248 at Broadford between Shalford and Peasmarsh and about 600yards from Shalford station. There is parking at the pub.

Approx. distance of walk: 3½ miles. Start at OS Map Ref. SU 998468.

The walk may be combined with Walk 16 at Point 3 and Walk 33 at Point 4.
A walk along the River Wey Navigation and across farmland. Do it in July for the wildflowers and the wildlife along the towpath.

1. Turn L out of the pub, cross the river and turn L on the towpath. Just past the second gate turn up R by an old bridge support onto a path, formerly the railway line. Just before a road bridge turn L on a path. Continue on a road and turn L into Oakdene Rd. Turn R at a pillar box, and cross the green and a road to a path to the L of a bus shelter.

2. Cross the railway via 2 stiles and bear R over a barrier and along a field edge to a track. Turn L past Brickfield Farm and its lovely lily pond. Turn R on a lane for ½ mile passing the entrance to Loseley Park and interesting old property, particularly the tiny church of St Francis, Littleton.

3. Opposite Pillarbox Cottage (Point 3 on Walk 16) turn R on a lane that narrows to a track then a path passing Mount Browne on the L. Join a road and turn L at a 'T' junction. Just past the bus stop on the R turn R past a barrier onto a track and under a railway arch.

4. Reach St Catherine's Lock (Point 2 on Walk 33) and turn R along the towpath, where in July swifts and damsel flies, whitethroats, reed warblers and goldfinches compete for your attention with the butterflies and wildflowers. At the road bridge turn up left back to the pub.

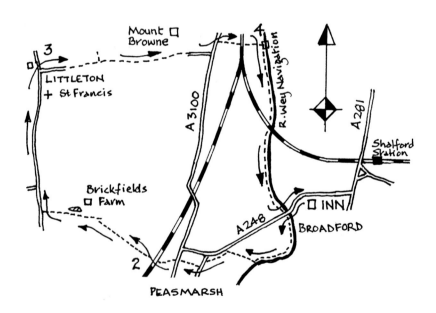

The Dog and Pheasant, Brook

The Dog and Pheasant, a former mediaeval hall house, is now a main road family pub with a separate restaurant and a tree house in the garden. Fortunately it manages to maintain the village pub atmosphere in the beamed bar areas. As we arrived the chef was picking fresh herbs from the garden.

Spirits were further uplifted by the sight of Ringwood's Boondoggle among the array of ales that also included Abbot, London Pride and Youngs bitter.

The pub specialises in fresh fish and home made pies e.g. braised beef and Ringwood ale pie. Other offerings include Thai chicken and prawn stir fry, bangers and mash, poached salmon salad and vegetarian Pad Thai. Snacks include jackets, baguettes and ploughman's and there is a children's menu.

Dogs are allowed in the bar and in the half of the garden not fenced off for children.

Opening hours are Mon-Fri 12-3pm and 5.30-11pm. Weekends all day from 12pm. Food is served all day at weekends.

Tel : 01428 685525.

Walk No. 10

The Dog and Pheasant at Brook is on the A286 between Milford and Haslemere. There is parking at the pub.

Approx. distance of walk: 5 miles. Start at OS Map Ref. SU 930381. The walk may be combined with Walk 25 at point 3.

An easy undulating walk over farmland with fine views at times and visiting the hamlet of Bowlhead Green. One short sharp hill.

1. Turn L out of the pub and take the first turning L. At Pine Lodge fork R through a kissing gate signed Greensand Way (GW)). Follow GW waymarks through woods and across fields with fine views. Cross the drive to Lower House and 2 more fields, then a lane. Turn R along a field edge to a stile, then between fields. Exit through a gate and over a lane still following GW waymarks. Cross a field and a track and go down through woods. At a 'T' junction turn R, then fork L down hill with steps at first. Turn R on a bridleway that may be wet, before passing between a pond and Cosford Farm.

2. At a fingerpost turn L on a bridleway leaving the GW. Pass a cottage and at a fingerpost turn L on a crossing path. This leads across the dam constructed to create the now disused fishpond on the R. Fork R on the drive to Blackhanger Farm, cross the stream and turn L over a stile. Bear half R past the corner of the garden and on to a stile in the corner of the field. Cross into a copse and emerge to bear half L up a long field. The path is clear and eventually leads you to a gate on the L. Advance to a waymark post by a grass path. This is Point 4 of Walk 25.

3. This section is common to Section 3 of Walk 25 in reverse. Continue to a stile into a bluebell wood, cross a sleeper bridge and a stile and then another stile into a field. Bear R to a stile by a gate and along a fenced path to a road.

4. Turn L on the road away from Walk 25 and at a signpost fork L for Bowlhead Green. Turn L up the drive to Blackhanger Farm and Halnacker Hill. Cross a stile on the R and over a field to another stile into woodland. Find out why Hal was (k)nackered as you scramble up the hill to a stile at the top, where we surprised a couple of fox cubs in a play fight. Go down the fields towards Emley Farm over 2 stiles and turn R on the track in front of the 16th century farm-

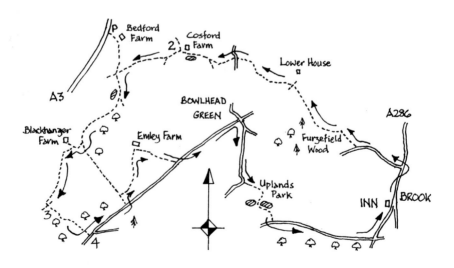

house. Back at the road turn L to the tiny hamlet of Bowlhead Green. You may be treated to the aroma of the countryside as you pass the farm but the houses are very attractive. Guess which one used to be a chapel. Turn R at the crossroads and at a fork go R uphill. About 15 yards past an arch bear L up to a stile and onto a fenced path. Turn R at the end of the field and R again onto a drive that leads between duck ponds and out through the two sets of gates to Uplands Park. Turn L on the road past more desirable properties and L again at the A286 back to the pub.

Emley Farm

Chapel Cottage at Bowlhead Green

The Half Moon, Charlwood

The Half Moon is a cosy welcoming local. The bar corner where Jim sits dates from the 15th century and other rooms have been added, one overlooking the churchyard, one at the front with pool, darts and machines and the dining room is an extension of the bar. Jim says the Sunday roasts (choice of 3) are the best quality and value around and so popular that the main menu is not available that day.

The ales are Bombardier, Old Speckled Hen and Young's Bitter.

The menu has a comprehensive range of sandwiches, baguettes, jackets, plough-man's and burgers. Main courses, all at £4 or £6.75 for 2 in August 2002, include pub mainstays such as bangers and mash, Cajun chicken, scampi, gammon, egg and chips and quorn based vegetarian dishes. There is a small garden, half given over to a well equipped children's playground.

Dogs on leads are welcome in the pub, which is open all day every day from 11.30am, (noon on Sunday).

Tel : 01293 862902.

Charlwood is reached from the A25 east of Dorking via Brockham and Leigh, or from the A217 and A24 north of Gatwick Airport via Hookwood. The Half Moon is in The Street, opposite St Nicholas Church. Parking is in the street.

Approx. distance of walk: 3½ miles. Start at OS Map Ref. TQ 242411. The walk may be combined with Walk 30 at Point 3.

A walk originally planned for the children incorporating the excellent and educational Gatwick Zoo. Our pleasure cannot be shared with you as, while there, we learned it was to close on 1 September 2002. This for a housing development to facilitate the migration of more of 'Two Jags' Prescott's relations from 'oop North' to the crowded South East. This modified farmland and woodland walk has bluebells or blackberries in season, a nature reserve and a special church interior. There may be mud in the woods.

1. Turn L out of the pub and through the churchyard. The 900 years old St Nicholas Church is usually open and has some fascinating mediaeval wall paintings. Continue on a path and turn R on Rectory Lane. As the road bends R turn L on the unsigned drive to Bristow's Cottage. Cross a stile and keep to the RH side of 3 fields over stiles to a road. Turn L on the footpath and L again at Beggarshouse Lane. Continue when this narrows to a path, the blackberries virtually jump into your mouth at one point. Pass under telegraph wires with Greenings Farm on the L and a view of Box Hill to the R.

2. At the entrance to a copse cross a sleeper bridge and stile on the L and bear L beside a ditch, then keep to the L hand side of 2 fields over a succession of stiles. At a fence corner in the next field bear half R to a circular trough and maintain direction to the bottom corner of the field. Cross a footbridge and stile and keep L across the field to turn L on Cidermill Road for 80 yards. Turn L at a bridleway fingerpost. At a fork just inside a bluebell wood keep ahead on the wide path.

3. At a path junction turn sharp L on the first waymarked footpath. This is point 3 on Walk 30 and Glover's Wood, a nature reserve. Do not deviate from this direct path through the wood, down steps and over Welland Gill and on for ½ mile. A notice board near the end tells you what you might have seen, before you emerge via a kissing gate and between fields to a private road. There is a novel garden ornament on the R. Continue along Glover's Road and cross Rectory Lane and retrace your outward path through the churchyard and back to the pub.

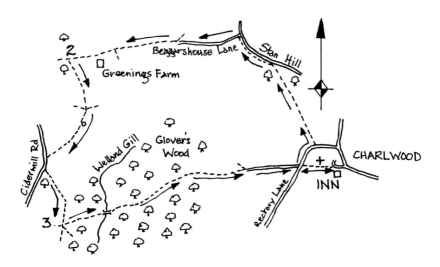

The Crown, Chiddingfold

The Crown, dating from 1285, is an impressive establishment with well furnished rooms, suntrap courtyards and tables along the frontage beneath the half timbered façade.

Hall and Woodhouse ownership ensures Tanglefoot is always available, even in the beer batter, along with Badger Best and Sussex bitter. There is a choice of 6 wines by the glass.

Lunchtime snacks include sandwiches, ploughman's, hot ciabattas and moules mariniéres, with more substantial fare such as liver and bacon, vegetable curry, warm Cajun chicken salad and salmon and prawn fusilli.

There is a superior restaurant and 8 letting rooms including some with four posters.

The pub is open all day every day and lunch is served from 12-2.30pm.

Children are not allowed in the bar areas and dogs are not allowed in the restaurant, so if you are blessed with both bring separate leads.

Tel : 01428 682255.

The Crown, Chiddingfold, is situated on the A283 Petworth Road, opposite St Mary's church and the village green. Car parking is beside the green.

Approx. distance of walk: 4 miles. Start at OS Map Ref. SU 961354.

A walk in the former centre of Britain's glass making industry, over farmland and through bluebell woods, with a route finding challenge on Forestry Commission land. There may be mud in the woods. The walk may be combined with Walk 32 at Point 3.

1. Turn R out of the pub. At a crossroads go forward into Pockford Road passing some lovely old cottages. Opposite Solars cross a stile, then a meadow diagonally to another stile. Maintain direction across a field and past a waymarked barrier, through a short section of woods and another field. At a waymarked post bear half R across the next field, through a gap in the hedge and straight across the next meadows. Go ahead at a fingerpost into a bluebell wood. In 20 yards turn R at a 'T' junction and at the next 'T' junction turn L with a river on the R. Follow the river out of the woods and along the edge of a field. Cross a footbridge and in a few yards at a 'T' junction turn L. At a fork go R uphill into woods, soon aided by steps. Look out for deer here and orchids in June. Follow a line of telegraph poles out to a road.

2. Turn R and in 60 yards L at a fingerpost. Keep to the L and at a fingerpost go L beside a fence. The path bends R past a Forestry Commission board and on to a sleeper bridge, then down steps to a gravel track. Turn R, cross a footbridge and continue uphill. Take the first turning R. The track bends R and you turn R at a waymark post.

Pick your way forward over the ruts to join a faint grass path forking R. At a 'T' junction in a few yards turn L. The path is barely discernible but maintain direction NW to cross an old brick footbridge and on uphill to a barrier near the corner of a field. Continue with the field to your R. Orchids line the path in June and you reach the lovely streamside setting of Corner Farm. Join a tarmac drive where a friendly pig may ask to have her tummy tickled and turn L at the road.

3. Reach a 'T' junction. You can turn L here past Corrie Mead to Point 2 of Walk 32. Otherwise head up the drive of Old Pickhurst opposite and turn R over a stile by the gate, then L before a gate. Keep to the field edge then bear R between gates. At the next field corner pass a waymarked stile into woods. Cross 2 footbridges with a pond to the L, the site of a former glassworks. Cross a stile and bear R round a field edge to exit over another stile and downhill into woods. Cross a stile and maintain direction with a fence on the L at first then a narrow copse. A final stile leads to a path past houses, then turn R on the road back to the pub.

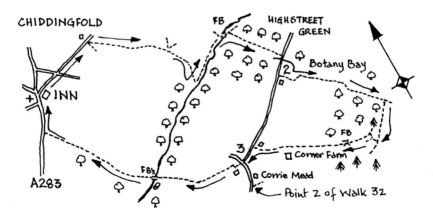

The Percy Arms, Chilworth

The Percy Arms, dating from the 18th Century, once served the workers from the nearby gunpowder factory and was used as a temporary mortuary when this blew up in 1901. One of these spirits was reluctant to leave the pub but you will only be bothered by his ghost if you quaff too much Greene King Abbot, Triumph or IPA ale. Popular with walkers this is a spacious family pub, with a conservatory and a large riverside garden with play space.

The extensive menu includes sandwiches, plain and toasted, jacket potatoes, tagliatelli verdi, various steaks in various sizes, haddock in beer batter, steak and kidney pie and char grilled pork escalope on lime and ginger noodles and Thai fish cakes among many others.

The pub is open all day every day.

Dogs in the garden only please.

Tel : 01483 561765.

The Percy Arms is situated on the A248 at Chilworth, reached via Albury, south from the A25. There is parking at the pub, which is opposite Chilworth Railway Station.

Approx. distance of walk: 4 miles. Start at OS Map Ref. TQ 031473.

The walk may be combined with Walk 2 at point 4 or Walk 33 at point 3 – see text of walk 33 – or Walk 7 – see map. A walk commencing on a riverside path, rising across farmland and through a bluebell wood to the little church of St Martha high on the N Downs Way with superb views, returning via the Downs Link.

1. Turn R out of the pub and R on 'Vera's Path' past the school. Cross a bridge over the R. Tillingbourne and turn L through the site of a former gunpowder factory. Ignore side paths and pass a fish pond over to the R to exit through a gate by an Information Board. Turn R on a lane and at Halfpenny Corner go L on a signed footpath.
2. At Halfpenny Lane again turn L through a gate and bear L between fields. Pass farm buildings and cross a stile on the R to bear R uphill through a field. Cross a stile and fork R then take the central path of 3 steeply uphill. At a crossing track turn R across a wildflower meadow with fine views bearing L to exit beside a gate. Fork L through a bluebell wood and pass a campsite on the R. Maintain direction at a junction of paths and

go over 2 crossing paths and past a barrier before a house.
3. At Halfpenny Lane turn L and in 30 yards turn R on a path signed N Downs Way. Cross the drive to Southernway and follow the sandy path, ignoring all side paths, up St Martha's Hill. Pass the church and turn R along the cemetery wall. Half way down turn L on a path between low fences. Ignore side paths to reach a N Downs Link board. Turn sharp right here downhill following Downs Link signs. At a 'T' junction turn L and cross the river.
4. If you want to combine with Walk 2 continue ahead here. Otherwise turn R through a barrier and fork L. At a 'T' junction turn R and at a picnic area fork L to cross the river and retrace your steps back to the pub.

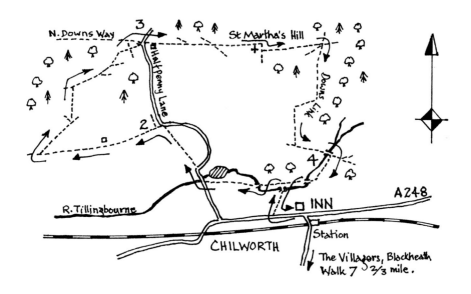

The Crossways Inn, Churt

This CAMRA award winning free house is to southwest Surrey what The Royal Oak, Wood Street is to northwest Surrey. Always welcoming and busy, the hub of the village offering good value pub food in traditional surroundings and with eight properly kept ales and four draft ciders. The ales change all the time, although Cheriton Best and Village Elder seem to be regulars. They are chalked on a board above the bar and the real ale devotees study this 'menu' before ordering, usually in half pints to widen the tasting opportunity. Our visit followed a beer festival week and there were still 20 to choose from, most of which were new to me. Fortunately we had already completed the walk.

The menu offers sandwiches, 4 ploughman's, homemade specials, steaks, gammon, chilli, quiche, chicken kiev, etc. and food is served from 12-2pm daily but NB not Sundays.

Dogs are welcome but children under 10 in the garden only.

Hours are Monday – Thursday 11am-3pm and 5-11pm, Friday and Saturday 11am-11pm. Sunday 12-4pm and 7-10.30pm.

Tel : 01428 714323.

The Crossways Inn is at the crossroads in the centre of Churt on the A287 Hindhead to Farnham road. There is parking at the pub.

Approx. distance of walk: 3½ miles. Start at OS Map Ref. SU 855382.

An undulating woodland walk along the county border through Whitmoor Vale; out in Surrey back in Hampshire. If you have time visit the main Miscellanea shop near the pub for a few things you couldn't live without, particularly the double throne khazi francais for the ultimate in togetherness.

1. Cross the A287 into Churt Road signed to Headley. Opposite the pumping station turn L uphill and at a fork go R passing Barford Mill with a stream down on the R. Where the track bends R to cottages keep ahead on a grass path with a pond on the R. Maintain direction on a drive and bear R at a road. After 200 yards by Woodland View turn R at a fingerpost down to cross a stream (the county border) and uphill again to a road.
2. Turn L and note the vegetable cage in the garden of Grey Cottage, proof that the woods are home to many deer. A quiet approach should bring its rewards. 100 yards past Dingley Dell fork R at a fingerpost uphill into woods. Turn R on a crossing path before a barrier and in 50 yards R again on a path through a pinewood. At a 'T' junction turn L to reach a gate onto a road. Turn R before the gate following the fingerpost downhill and after 25 yards fork L. The path goes between fences to reach the drive to Walnut Well. Do not advance to the road but cross the drive and turn L uphill. Bear R at a small wooden gate and then keep beside a fence as it bends L to a road via the drive of Cobwebs.
3. Turn R for 100 yards then turn L over a stile by a gate into woodland. In a few yards fork R. The path becomes sunken between fields and you pass some badger earthworks before joining a farm drive. Turn R on Churt Rd back to the pub.

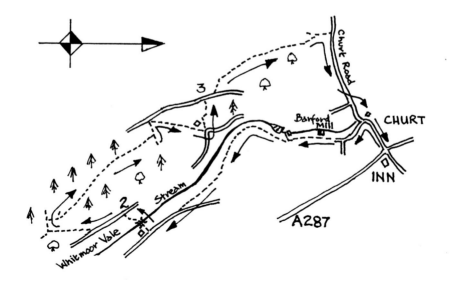

37

The Plough, Coldharbour

You are already half way to heaven in the heights of Coldharbour and real ale drinkers will enter the Pearly Gates to the bar of the Plough. Tanglefoot, Timothy Taylor's The Landlord, Ringwood Old Thumper and Sussex bitter are supplemented by 3 of landlord Rick Abrehart's own Leith Hill Brewery offerings. Try the excellent Crooked Furrow or Tallywhacker.

There is an attractive restaurant and two bars linked by a central fire. They are small for a pub often overflowing with walkers and the rear garden is tiny. However, reminiscent of continental vineyards, there is a barn with tables and an open fire in winter to cater for the overspill.

The menu offers six ploughman's, jackets and roast lunches every day together with homemade favourites like steak and ale pie. There is a children's menu and dogs on leads are welcome in the bars.

Hours are 11am-3pm and 6-11pm on weekdays and all day at weekends.

Tel : 01306 711793.

The Plough is in the centre of Coldharbour and can be reached by turning south off the A25 on Coldharbour Lane in Dorking or Hollow Lane in Wotton. Alternatively from the A29 turn north on Broomehall Rd one mile north of Ockley. There is very limited car parking outside the pub but there are 2 car parks in Abinger Road – see map.

Approx. distance of walk: 3½ miles. Start at OS Map Ref. TQ 152441.

The walk may be combined with Walk 20 at Point 2. A walk in the forest passing a beautiful pond before a gentle ascent along the Greensand Way to the panoramic views from Leith Hill. From the highest hill in the county you pass the highest cricket pitch on your way back to the highest pub.

1. Cross the road to the signed byway opposite. Fork L before a gate and at a junction of tracks take the first L. At a fork keep R and at the next junction bear R between posts then turn R downhill. Stay on this track ignoring L and R forks to pass Tilling Springs and the photogenic pond resplendent with swans and water lilies in July. At a 'T' junction turn L on the Greensand Way (GW). This section is common to walk 20, as far as the fingerpost opposite Warren Farm, where Walk 20 turns right.

2. Continue past a waymarked gate and stay on this track gently uphill for almost 1 mile. At a major junction of 5 tracks turn R, still on the GW, up to Leith Hill Tower. You are 965ft above sea level and if you go up the viewing tower, once used as a smugglers lookout, you will top the 1000ft. Opening hours can be obtained from the National Trust 01306 712434 or 711777.

3. Retrace your steps to the track junction and take the second on the R uphill then fork R at the red arrow waymark. Go over a wide crossing track and immediately after passing 4 posts across the track turn L. Ignore two L forks and at a junction of minor paths keep ahead past the yellow arrow. Go over a crossing path and with Coldharbour cricket pitch to your L bear R on a wide track back to the pub. Near the road we were surprised by a nightingale singing at full volume.

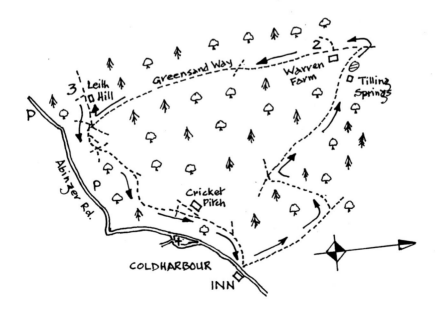

39

The Harrow, Compton

Outwardly The Harrow is a nondescript looking pub on a busy road through a pretty village desperately in need of a by-pass. Inside this 300 year old inn reveals its character in nicely furnished beamed rooms, a cheery welcome and Hogs Back TEA to slake the thirst, along with Pedigree and Greene King IPA. There are 8 wines available by the glass.

The blackboard menu is extensive and imaginative. In addition to traditional pub fare like ploughman's, steak and ale pie and fresh cod in beer batter, there are the likes of nasi goreng, pork and cider casserole, warm chicken, bacon and avocado salad and red snapper on a corn and tomato salsa garnished with peppers. After that try the 'chocolate junkyard' if you dare.

The pub is child and dog friendly (water bowls supplied).

Go there for breakfast before starting out as the hours are 8am-11pm Monday - Saturday and 8am-6pm Sunday. Lunch is served 12-2.30pm and 6-10pm.

There are 6 en-suite rooms.

Tel : 01483 810379.

The Harrow is situated on the B3000 turning off the A3 about 2½ miles SW of Guildford. There is parking at the pub.

Approx. distance of walk: 5 miles. Start at OS Map Ref. SU 956469.

The walk may be combined with Walk 9 at Point 3.

A varied walk with a historic church and artistic interest at the start, a section of the N Downs Way then farmland, a pond and a bluebell wood. The last section has nettles or mud according to season but can be avoided by a short cut.

1. Turn L out of the pub and visit the little Norman church of St Nicholas. Information on the special features is available inside. There are other old properties to admire as you continue along the road. Turn R at Down Lane. The Watts Mortuary Chapel in the cemetery commemorates the Victorian artist George Frederick Watts and is worth a visit, as is the Watts Gallery further along Downs Lane where his works are exhibited. Tel 01483 810235 for opening times.

2. In front of the Watts Gallery fork R signed N Downs Way. Skylarks sing and bluebells line your path and at a crossing track go ahead into the Loseley Estate Nature Reserve. Pass a fingerpost and follow N Downs Waymarks onto a wide sandy track. At a crossing track turn R joining Littleton Lane.

3. At Pillarbox Cottage (Point 3 on Walk 9)

turn R. Maintain direction over several stiles passing a lovely pond with Loseley House beyond. Cross a track and stile and follow the path round to the left over two more stiles. Turn R at a 'T' junction on a wide path between fields.

4. At a lane by Little Polsted, if you are not dressed for mud or nettles according to season, you can take the road left back to the pub – follow dotted arrows on map. Otherwise turn R on a path and in 50 yards turn L up steps onto an enclosed path. Cross a stile and a field to another, where turn L to skirt a bluebell wood. Cross a stile to enter woodland and at a junction of paths go ahead on the widest one. Fork L soon with a fence on your L and at a road turn R. Just past Almsgate on the R turn R across grass and join the main road back to the pub.

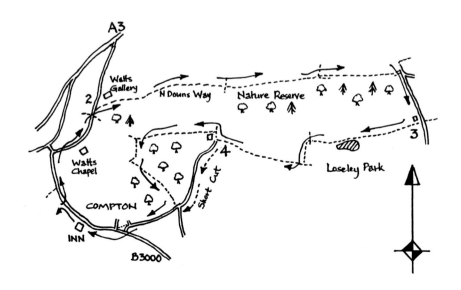

The Sun, Dunsfold

The Sun is an atmospheric welcoming local, part of it formerly an old barn dating back to the 15th century. The dining room has an inglenook and outside there is a patio and tables on the common.

The cosy bar offers four ales, Adnams Broadside and Bitter, Sussex and Ansells Bitter and a good selection of wines. There is a choice of 10 cigars if it is your birthday.

The very extensive blackboard menu includes reasonably priced sandwiches and baguettes and various ploughman's, as well as serious fare like steak, ale and mushroom pie, rack of lamb and grilled whole sea bass in lemon and lime salsa. There is a separate children's menu and well behaved dogs are welcome.

Hours are 11am-11pm daily, Sunday 12-10.30pm. Food is served from 12-2.15pm, Sunday 12-3pm and 7-9.30pm.

Tel : 01483 200242.

Dunsfold is about 4 miles SW of Cranleigh, reached by a turning off the B2130. The Sun is set back from the road behind common land. Car parking is beside the common.

Approx. distance of walk: 3½ miles. Start at OS Map Ref. TQ 006361.

A walk through a bluebell wood and across farmland with fine views and a visit to an immaculate ancient church. The section after the church may be muddy.

1. Go forward from the pub to cross the main road, turn L then R at a fingerpost by the Baptist Church. Pass a pond and follow the lane round to pass gallops and enter woodland. Cross a footbridge and continue uphill with a bluebell wood to your L to reach a lane. Turn L for ½ mile and pass a pond.

2. At a fingerpost turn L into High Loxley Farm. Go through a gate, turn L then R through a small wooden gate. Bear L to cross a stile in the corner of the field and turn R through the second gate on the R. This is a sheep farm and I was asked to stress the importance of shutting gates and keeping dogs on leads. Head down the field beside the fence. There are fine views of Hascombe Hill and Hydons Ball to the R and Blackdown ahead. Go through a gate and across a field, over a stile to a fenced path and on to a road. Cross the road and turn L then R at a fingerpost. Pass 2 lily ponds and just past Eden Cottage turn R through a gate, then fork L, soon beside a wooden fence on our R. Go through a gate, down to a stream and steeply uphill to a wooden

gate. Go ahead along the RH edge of a field and over a stile into Hookhouse Road.

3. Turn R then L at a fingerpost onto a concrete drive. Just before gates on both sides turn L over a waymarked stile into a field. Follow the field edge down and left along the bottom to cross a stile in the corner. Bear half R across a field to a stile into a churchyard. Dating from 1260, St Mary and All Saints is usually open and the guide is £1 well spent. Outside the hollow yew tree is thought to be 1000 years old and swifts nest above the porch. A place to linger before heading out through the yew arch and turning right to the Holy Well. Supposedly good for eye diseases I think I would want to filter and boil the water first! Continue past the well on a path beside a stream. Cross a footbridge, stroke the donkey and turn R then L, now with the stream on your L. Cross the stream again and the messy bridleway bends L uphill to join a residential road. At a fingerpost turn L down a gravel drive, over a stile and along a path to a kissing gate. Continue along the road and turn R at a 'T' junction back to the pub.

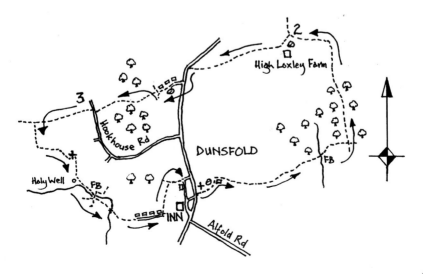

43

The Mill, Elstead

The handsome 4 storey Elstead Mill begs to be photographed from every angle. It is built over the River Wey with outside tables over the water and in the lovely garden, where grey wagtails wag and swans, Canada geese and mallard may demand your bread. The bar is on the ground floor where there is a working mill wheel and the brasserie is upstairs. Outside is a terrain for petanque and boules may be hired from the bar.

The ales are TEA and their own Elstead, both by Hogs Back, and there is a choice of wines by the glass.

The menu offers sandwiches, ploughman's, four salads including duck breast and delicious ham and e.g. fresh haddock in beer batter, baby pork ribs, homemade pie of the day and vegetarian risotto.

Children are welcome but guide dogs only.

Hours 12-11pm and food is served from 12-3pm and 6-9pm Monday to Saturday and 12-4pm and 5.30-8pm Sunday.

Tel : 01252 703333.

Elstead Mill is on the B3001 Milford to Farnham road just west of the village. There is ample parking.

Approx. distance of walk: 4½ miles. Start at OS Map Ref. SU 904438.

A walk with a bit of everything – riverside with ancient bridges and damselflies, farmland, woodland with bluebells and deer, lakeside with des.res. and the village green with more des.res.

1. Leave the Mill along the drive, turn R at the road and cross to a fingerpost before the bridge. The path goes beside the R.Wey where multi coloured damselflies skim over the water and the Himalayan balsam plants in July. Cross a footbridge and a stile. The path leaves the river and goes across 2 more sleeper bridges and beside wooden buildings to a barrier and on to a road. Turn R, pass Fullbrook House and turn R on an unsigned track. Look out for a wooden gate on the L and follow the fingerpost direction across a field to another gate into a copse. Cross a footbridge and reach a road.

2. Turn L then bear R on a bridleway just past the entrance to Cutmill Cottage. Look out for deer here. The 3 we saw were big and unusually bold. Go over a wide track and across the end of Cutmill Pond. The small pond on the R in the grounds of Cutmill House is covered in kingcups in July.

Bear L towards the boathouse then R on the drive to Garden and Willow Cottages. Join the path into woodland to the R of a wooden garage and listen out for woodlarks. At a road turn R towards Rodsall Manor and R again on a signed bridleway. At a 'T' junction turn R downhill. Ignore 2 L turns, join a drive by Kingshott Cottage and bear L to a road.

3. Turn L through Gatwick and at a junction turn R signed Elstead. Just past Horseshoe Cottage on the R turn R through a gate. Pass a house and where the track turns R keep ahead with a fence on your R. Where the fence ends bear L to find a waymarked path into woods. Cross a footbridge and pass a pillbox and soon you will see the river on your R. Battle through a patch of bracken to a stile and cross a field to the corner of Somerset Bridge.

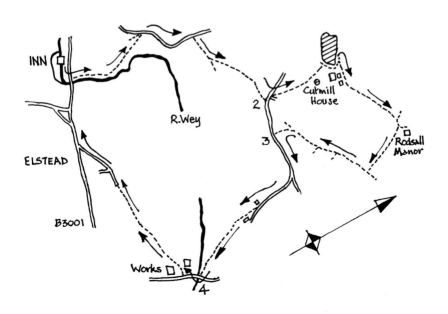

4. Cross the bridge and turn R into the works entrance. Pass a barrier and join a footpath to the L of metal double gates. Maintain direction as the path becomes a track then a residential road. Keep ahead on Ham Lane and turn R on the B3001. Pass the village green, 2 pubs and some interesting property and over Elstead Old Bridge back to The Mill.

Elstead Mill

The Windmill, Ewhurst

Ewhurst is blessed with 2 fine pubs, both on this walk. The Windmill is featured because of the unrivalled view from their conservatory and garden. A through fire warms both bar and dining area in winter and the whole is decorated with farming and hunting artefacts, although the stuffed birds and dismembered fox lower the tone.

The ales are not bad either – Hogs Back TEA and Hop Garden Gold, London Pride and Greene King IPA. A much wider choice will be available if you select for your visit the weekend of their annual beer festival.

There is an excellent menu with a good choice of salads, ploughman's, jackets and sandwiches, plain and toasted. The specials are imaginative e.g. broccoli and walnut soup, shark steak, braised rabbit and lamb kofta kebabs. Children can have smaller portions of adult meals and dogs are welcome and may share the resident's water bowl.

The pub is open all day every day from noon with food served from 12-2pm (2.30pm Sunday) and 7-9.30pm except Mondays.

Tel : 01483 277566.

Walk No. 19

The Windmill is on Shere Road about 1 mile north of Ewhurst centre. Turn south off the A25 signed Shere and follow signs for Ewhurst for 4 miles. There is parking at the pub and in a public car park nearby.

Approx. distance of walk: 4½ miles. Start at OS Map Ref. TQ 080424.

A walk over farmland and through bluebell woods, culminating in a fairly strenuous climb to the summit of Pitch Hill rewarded with fine views. There may be mud on the bridleways.

1. Turn L out of the pub up the road. Opposite the public car park turn L at a fingerpost on a drive and through a waymarked gate. Fork L past Ewhurst windmill then fork R on the Greensand Way (GW). At the net fork keep L down to a road, where turn L for ½ mile passing Winterfold House on the R. Just past Three Hatches turn L at a fingerpost and cross a garden field into a copse. Bear R to a bridleway below and cross a footbridge. Bluebells line the path that soon bends L. Ignore a stile on the L and at a waymarked fork go L, and continue on this bridleway.

2. Just past Wykehurst Farm turn R at a fingerpost. This enclosed path leads up steps and over a stile, soon with Coneyhurst Gill below L and the sloping bank covered with bluebells. Cross a stile and turn L on a road for 500 yards to reach Ewhurst opposite The Bull's Head. Turn L into Shere Road and in 100 yards turn R at a fingerpost into a copse. Cross a stile into a field and keep to the LH edge to exit over a footbridge.

Continue to a stile and uphill in woods. Keep beside the hedge on the L to reach a stile.

3. Cross into a field and bear half R to another stile. Turn R on a road and take the path to the L of a gate. Fork R over a stile and along the LH side of a field. Keep beside the fence as it bends L and maintain direction over a stile and through a kissing gate. Cross diagonally L to a field corner and turn L on a track. Turn R at a road and fork L past Little Stabling. The road bends L and in 25 yards turn R on a footpath uphill, then fork L more steeply uphill. Cross a lane following the GW waymark, pass a seat on your L with fine views and take the second path on the L with wooden safety barriers. Keep L and at a fork 20 yards before another seat turn sharp R to the summit of Pitch Hill, where there is a toposcope to help you identify the views. Pass the trig. point on your L and go downhill to the car park where turn L on the road back to the pub.

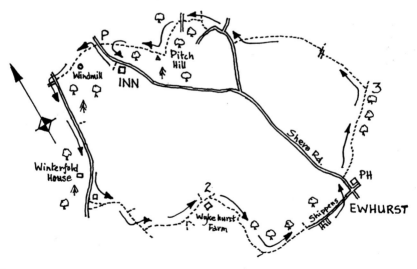

Ewhurst Windmill

The Stephan Langton, Friday Street

Stephan Langton, from these parts, was Archbishop of Canterbury and a draughtsman and signatory of the Magna Carta in 1215. I have been a customer at this popular walkers pub on and off for 45 years and found it much changed. 'Ponsified' was the verdict of one group with hairy legs and bedrolls furiously heading for the Abinger Hatch. It is true that the specials blackboard is now a wine list and you may need a translator for pork confit, morcilla, chorizo and butterbeans or roast cod, cockles, puy lentils and gremolata. Nevertheless the food is nicely cooked and beautifully presented. Those in doubt opted for the baps (panini) and the toaster was working full time. Oh, and amongst the exotica were calves liver and bacon and Cumberland sausage, mash and onion gravy.

Adnams bitter and London Pride were available. The sun came out and Billy Holiday was on the soundtrack. First impressions sometimes need drinking over!

Children and dogs on leads are welcome.

Opening hours are Mon-Sat 11am-4.30pm and 7-11pm. Sun 12-4.30pm and 7-10.30pm.

Tel : 01306 730775.

Friday Street is reached by turning south off the A25 on Hollow Lane, half a mile west of Wotton and taking the first signposted left turn. Just past a free public car park turn R beside a pond to the Stephan Langton, where parking is limited.

Approx. distance of walk: 3½ miles. Start at OS Map Ref. TQ 128456.

A walk through the Wotton Estate on woodland tracks and paths passing a water-fall in the Tillingbourne valley. Section 2 is the same as Section 2 of Walk 40 and point 4 is common to Point 2 of Walk 15.

1. Turn R out of the pub and R across the end of the millpond and uphill. Where the road bends R join the drive to Kempslade Farm and bear L to a stile and path.
2. At a 'T' junction turn R and R again at an immediate fork, now with a field to your R. Cross a lane via kissing gates and go ahead, soon steeply downhill in woods. Bear L over a stile and cross the river.
3. At a stile turn R on a track with the Tillingbourne below. Pass a pretty waterfall and turn L at a road by a Riding Centre, then in a few yards L again on a signed bridleway. At a fork keep R on the main track. Pass Pond Cottage, ignore paths to L and R and at a fork keep R.
4. Opposite Warren Farm is a fingerpost. Turn R here uphill, then bear left between large beech trees. The path is indistinct here but keep left and it reappears. Bear R on a track at a waymark post and Turn R at a fingerpost, soon joining a wider path. Ignore a L turn and go L at a fork. At a junction of tracks take the second on the R up to a road.
5. Cross half L to a fingerpost and down through woods and across a field to a kissing gate. Pass houses and look out for guinea fowl in the field on the R. The path descends to Abinger Bottom where turn R before a waymark post. Turn L on a road and opposite the last house bear R on a bridleway. Ignore a footbridge on the R and keep on the dry ground between the bridleway and the stream, eventually past houses and back to the pub.

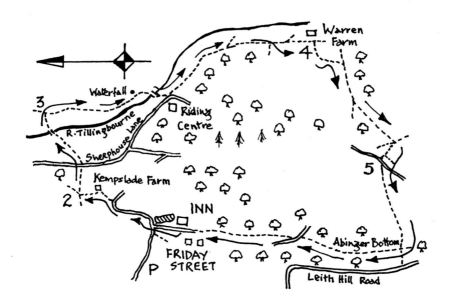

The Manor Inn, Godalming

Originally a manor house, The Manor Inn and Hotel is a sprawling family pub on the main road to Guildford belonging to the 'Out and Out' chain. Cosy it is not but the service is cheerful and efficient and it is popular with the boating fraternity. The pub's best feature is the riverside garden with a well equipped playground.

Ales available are Wadsworth's 6X, London Pride and Flowers Original and there is a selection of wines by the glass.

The reasonably priced menu is extensive, includes a children's section and is served all day every day from "noon 'til late". Examples are vegetable samosas, fresh fish and chips, lamb Koftas, Thai fish cakes, four cheese pasta, Stilton, pear and walnut salad and various steaks.

16 en-suite rooms

Tel: 01483 427134.

The Manor Inn is situated on the south side of the A3100, Guildford Rd, about 1 mile NE of Godalming town centre. There is a large car park at the pub.

Approx. distance of walk: 4 miles. Start at OS Map Ref SU 984450.

A walk that starts along the R Wey Navigation and then meanders through the hills east of Godalming, mostly on bridle paths that may be muddy. You should see pot bellied pigs and bluebells in season.

1. Leave the pub through the garden and turn R on the towpath. At Farncombe Boat House turn L on the road over the Wey Navigation and the R Wey. As the road bends R bear L across the grass verge to join Catteshall Rd. Cross Warramil Rd and at a 'T' junction turn L. The house in front of you used to be The Ram, one of the finest real ale and cider pubs in Surrey. Go R here then L on a lane by a bridleway fingerpost. Pass Catteshall Farm entrance and continue on this hillside path for ½ mile.

2. Opposite Lane Cottage is Violet Wood, apparently open to the public and a lovely spot to stroll around or sit awhile. Continue to a road and turn L then R at Orchards, where we watched a goldcrest tugging spider's web from a crevice in the wall to make its nest. Fork L on a footpath, cross a stile by a gate then a stile between gates. Maintain direction over a stile, now with fine views, then downhill over more stiles to a farm and road.

3. Turn L then L again on a signed bridleway uphill. Fork R by Orchard Cottage to reach a road where turn L. Just past the entrance to Priory, Unsted Park, turn R on a signed bridleway. At a gate keep ahead on the bridleway and at a junction by a blue kissing gate take the central path downhill. Ignore side turnings to the R to reach a crossing track, where turn R briefly, then L beside the pot bellied pigs. Cross the R Wey and turn R back to the pub.

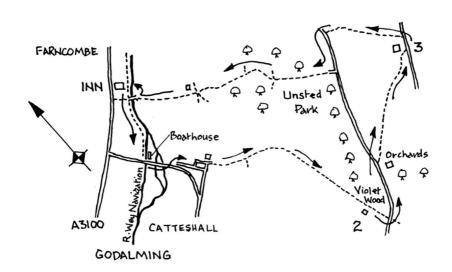

The Wheatsheaf, Grayswood

The Wheatsheaf free house is an attractive welcoming pub with a smart conservatory dining room and a floral patio garden.

The ales featured are Ringwood's Boondoggle and Bitter and Timothy Taylor's The Landlord plus Fullers ESB and London Pride. There is a selection of wines by the glass.

Service was cheerful and brisk on a busy Sunday. Along with traditional roasts the menu offered British style food but with very original presentation, e.g. grilled whole plaice, lambs liver and bacon, avocado and prawn salad, chicken leek and bacon pie and carrot, orange and coriander quiche. Snacks included 3 'rustic' cheese ploughman's, open toasted sandwiches and the Huntsman's sandwich of rib-eye steak and onion salad.

Children are welcome except in the bar and dogs on leads except in the restaurant. There are 7 en-suite rooms.

Opening hours are Monday – Saturday 11am–3pm and 6-11pm, Sunday 12-3pm and 7-10.30pm.

Tel: 01428 644440.

The Wheatsheaf is on the A286 at Grayswood about 1 mile north of Haslemere. There is parking at the pub.

Approx. distance of walk: 5½ miles. Start at OS Map Ref. SU 916345.

A walk on farmland, on quiet lanes, through woods and past tranquil ponds with an industrial past. You may encounter deer and mud in the woods.

1. Turn L out of the pub down to All Saints Church. It was designed by a Swedish architect and his sail shaped headstone in the churchyard depicts a Viking ship. Cross the road into Lower Road and at a fork keep L. At a 'T' junction with Clammer Hill cross over and continue on a track bearing R past the gate to a sewage plant. Go through a gate and bear R down a meadow with a fence on your L. Go through a copse and bear half L across the next field, then along the field edge. Cross another field and turn L at the fingerpost at the end. Keep to the field edge, where you may see yellowhammers and redstarts and enter woods. Fork L at a waymark post. At a fingerpost keep ahead, continue over a footbridge and uphill past a waymark post and over a stile. Maintain direction along a field edge before bearing half L to a stile. Then aim to the L of farm buildings to another stile. Turn R on the drive of Frillinghurst Farm out to a lane.
2. Turn R for ½ mile and at a 'T' junction turn R for another ½ mile before turning R at a fingerpost through the gates to Furnace Place. In the 16th and 17th centuries

Imbhams Iron Foundry was sited here using power from the ponds to run a boring mill making, among other things, cannon barrels. Pass Stream House, cross a bridge and bear L, then fork L signed for Stable Cottage. The track enters a woodland fringe. Look out for a grass path on the L opposite a field entrance that is a short detour to a pond of interest to bird and dragonfly watchers.
3. At a junction keep ahead passing another large pond on your L. Look out for dabchicks here. Follow the track round to the L into Imbhams Farm entrance, where bear R to a grass path with a fence on the L. Enter a bluebell wood and fork L uphill. Exit through a gate onto a fenced path, reach a road and turn R. Just past Clammer Hill Cottage turn L over a stile onto a fenced path, then through a kissing gate. Bear R to a seat and kissing gate and uphill to a stile in the top LH corner of a meadow. The path leads under a tunnel and down 2 flights of steps to a road. Turn R and where the road ends continue on a track to reach the A286. Cross and turn R back to the pub.

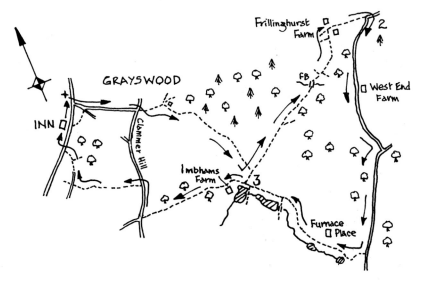

The Merry Harriers, Hambledon

The landlord reveals his 'Merry' side with roadside boards offering 'warm beer and lousy food'. Locals know better of course but I have often wondered about the effectiveness of this sort of advertising in drawing in the passing trade. Fear not the ales, Hogs Back TEA and Hop Back Crop Circle, were served in perfect condition. Greene King Abbot and IPA also feature regularly.

The good selection of hot and cold 'pub grub' was reasonably priced for Surrey, the atmosphere welcoming and the service cheery. Ancients and over indulgers suffering the disturbance of having to get up in the night, will be interested in the fine collection of Victorian chamber pots raised from under the bed for display on the ceiling. In the garden 9 feeders attract hosts of birds. We counted 14 species including nuthatch, bullfinch, goldfinch and coal tit.

Opening times are weekdays 11am-3pm and 6-11pm, with lunchtime extensions to 4pm at weekends.

Dogs are welcome; children "on a lead only".

Tel: 01428 682883.

The Merry Harriers is situated in Hambledon Road, north of the village. Take the turning off the A283 south of Wormley signed Hambledon and follow signs for 1 mile. There is parking in front and opposite the pub.

Approx. distance of walk: 3½ miles. Start at OS Map Ref. SU 967391.

The walk takes you past ponds and wildflower meadows and climbs gently up to Hydon's Ball with fine views. The descent is through woods and across farmland passing a lovely church. This walk is not recommended for winter or after heavy rain. It can be joined with Walk 39, Witley, in a figure of eight.

1. Turn L out of the pub and immediately L again on a bridleway. The track bears L and you reach a sleeper bridge and turn R at a waymark post. At a junction of paths keep ahead and turn R at the next waymark and go over a crossing track. At the next waymark turn R and go through a gate.

2. This next section is common in the reverse direction to Walk 39. Head up the wildflower meadow with Enton Hall on your L and on your R a pond and marshy area, home to dabchicks.

3. Keep to the right and fork R through a barrier before a house. Cross a narrow stream and turn L on a path that leads out to a golf course. Turn L along the side of a fairway and down to a crossing path where turn R. Cross this and a second fairway keeping a wooden barn to your L. Maintain direction on this track to cross a road and join the bridleway opposite. Pass between fields and then climb through woods with a wire fence to your R. At a crossing track turn R, still with a fence on your R. Pass 2 wooden gates and, where the fence bears R,

turn L on a narrow path that leads you to the summit of Hydon's Ball. Note the monument to Octavia Hill one of the three founders of The National Trust. To descend retrace your steps to a fork and take the wider path on the L instead of the narrow one you came up on. Keep on this track steeply downhill ignoring side turnings to reach a crossing track.

4. Go ahead passing a pumping station on your right (If this track is very muddy there is a short cut to the church – see dotted arrows on map). At a 'T' junction turn R and immediately R again on the Greensand Way. There are lovely views over the fields to the North Downs and an interesting chestnut tree on "stilts" to the R. You reach St Peter's Church in its most attractive setting with substantial yew trees. If you turn sharp R before reaching the church there is an old lime kiln a few yards down on the R. Retrace your steps, pass the church and fork R at a fingerpost past Stable Cottage. This leads to a tree lined path going downhill back to the pub.

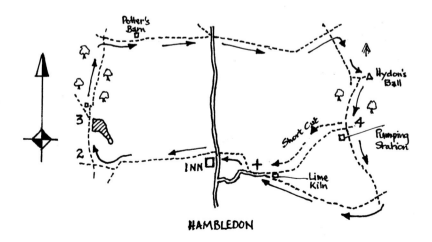

HAMBLEDON

The White Horse, Hascombe

Situated on the Greensand Way, The White Horse is an old coaching inn, parts of which date back to the 16th century. It is spacious with several beamed eating areas and a separate up market restaurant.

Adnams, Flowers and Harveys bitters are available and a selection of wines by the glass.

The menu is extensive and imaginative, for example, brie and asparagus tart, crispy duck wraps, Thai chicken salad, grilled guinea fowl. Outside there is a terrace and a large garden with 50 tables. We were entertained by dunnocks, tits and song thrushes rushing about feeding fledglings oblivious to the well fed cat asleep beneath my chair. Regardless of the cat the management welcomes dogs.

Children away from the bar area only.

Opening hours are : weekdays 11-3pm and 5.30-11pm, weekends open all day. Tel: 01483 208258.

The White Horse is situated on the B2130 Brighton Road, 3½ miles south of Godalming. There is parking at the pub.

Approx. distance of walk: 2½ miles, with an optional extension of a further 2½ miles. Start at OS Map Ref. TQ 002395.

Go on a fine day in May and this short walk gets you quickly up Hascombe Hill for fine views with time to linger with the bluebells before a rapid descent past the lovely village pond and church. There is an optional extension or afternoon stroll along lanes and woodland paths to the west of the village.

1. Turn L out of the pub and immediately L again on a bridleway. Turn R at a wooden garage and cross a stile onto a sunken track. At a fork keep L uphill and at the next fork go R among rhododendrons. At a junction of paths bear R circling the hill top, the site of an Iron Age fort. There are fine views over Dunsfold and Alfold. Ignore a turning L and at a fork go L, soon downhill between a field on the L and a bluebell wood.
2. At a 'T' junction turn R then first L through an avenue of trees. There are good views ahead to the N Downs and Nore Hanger is below you. At a fork keep R and at a 'T' junction turn L on a path. Take the next L turn and maintain the westerly direction on this path for ½ mile ignoring side turnings and eventually descend to a road. Keep ahead past the village pond and

church, an idyllic scene, and back to the pub.
3. To do the extended walk retrace your steps past the church and bear left on the road. Turn L on a bridleway before Upper House Farm. Cross a stile by a green gate and follow the path over two more stiles to rejoin the bridleway. Keep ahead past a farm and fork L before a blue gate. Cross a road and head uphill on the bridleway opposite. At a road turn L and at a 'T' junction L again.
4. Pass Hascombe Court and at a fork go L. Exit through a gate and just before a lane note Mr Fox's back gate at the foot of the fence. Cross the lane and continue on the bridleway ignoring paths off to the left. Enter woodland and in 80 yards at a crossing track turn L by a 'Walkers Welcome' waymark. At a fork keep ahead. The path

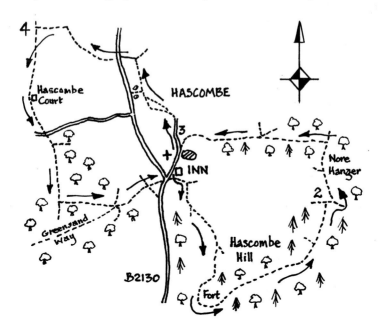

bends R to a crossing track. Go ahead to the Greensand Way (GW) marker post and bear L. In a few yards at the next GW waymark turn L and immediately fork L down a gully. At a fork continue to follow the GW steeply downhill to a stile on the L. Cross a field and another stile to reach a path. If the field ahead is not too boggy you are just 2 stiles from the pub. Those inadequately shod turn R on this path and left at the B2130. By the time you reach the pub 'Wonderful Walker' in the bright green wellies should have had time to get the first round in.

Hascombe Church

The Devil's Punchbowl

The Devil's Punchbowl Hotel, Hindhead

The Devil's Punchbowl Hotel, Steakhouse and Conference Centre is the only pub in Hindhead and tries to be all things to all men. The Russell Bar is reminiscent of a railway station bar with a nondescript soundtrack and a regular stream of transient builders, drivers and salesmen mixing with hotel guests. Walkers with well behaved dogs are also welcome. It is by no means cosy but the staff are pleasant and efficient.

The ales are Wadsworth's 6X, Ansells bitter and Bass and there is a choice of wines by the glass.

The food was good and reasonably priced e.g. children's menu offering a choice of 6 meals all at £2.95 in July 2002. The menu features organic Scotch beef steaks, hot chicken and salmon salads, salmon and tuna steaks, sandwiches and vegetarian dishes and best of all, for those straggling back late after scaling the rim of the Punchbowl, the food is served from 12-10pm daily.

Tel: 01428 606565.

Walk No. 25

The Devil's Punchbowl Hotel is situated on the southern side of the A3 at the eastern edge of Hindhead opposite a garage and large National Trust car park. The hotel has its own large car park.

Approx. distance of walk: 4 miles. Start at OS Map Ref. SU 889357. The walk may be combined with Walk 10 at Point 3.

A hilly walk commencing on the Greensand Way across Hindhead Common where bilberries grow and highland cattle graze. You visit the viewpoint on Gibbet Hill before diving down to farmland. The return is through the woods of Boundless Copse and the dramatic Devil's Punchbowl.

1. Turn R out of the pub and 25 yards past the end of the car park turn R at a finger post signed Greensand Way (GW). Keep on the well waymarked GW ignoring other paths for ½ mile. Look out for Highland cattle grazing in the heather and stonechats 'chatting' as you pass. At a fork by a seat go L (GW) and at a 'T' junction turn L and over a cattle grid. At a junction of tracks keep ahead (GW) and at the next fork before a small NT car park go R away from the GW and up to the viewpoint on Gibbet Hill, the second highest point in Surrey after Leith Hill.

2. Retrace your steps to the track junction and turn sharp left downhill. At a junction of 7 tracks maintain direction on the third exit left and at a fork go L on the deeply rutted track that soon gets muddy. You can avoid the mud by getting up in the woods on the L and soon a drainage channel improves the situation. Pass a cottage on the R and at a fingerpost keep R on the tarmac. Turn L before Creedhole Farm and maintain direction at the next junction.

3. About 45 yards before the road forks turn L at a fingerpost. This is point 4 of Walk 10 and this section is common to Section 3 of Walk 10 in reverse. Go through a gate onto a fenced path. Cross a stile into a meadow and continue to a stile in the LH fence. Cross into a bluebell wood and follow the path over a stile and sleeper bridge. Leave the woods over a stile by a gate and bear R to a waymark post.

4. Turn L away from Walk 10, pass a small pond and continue with a fence on the L. Cross a stile by a gate and maintain direction along the RH side of a field with Begley Farm on your right. Exit over a stile onto a road, turn R then L at a fingerpost. Pass a barrier and go uphill over a crossing track, then another. The path gets narrower and steeper as you rise to the A3.

5. Cross carefully to a fingerpost and bear L on the NT path. At a lane turn R downhill then at a waymark post by a yellow grit bin turn sharp L, soon through a kissing gate. Keep on this track down hill over 3 crossing tracks and soon you are on a switchback of dips and rises. At a fork just past a boggy area go R soon with steps to aid you. At the top turn R and you can rest on a seat with a superb view of the Punchbowl and beyond. Go through a kissing gate and in a few yards fork L then R to the NT car park and across the A3 back to the hotel.

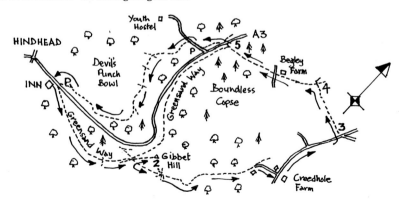

The Royal Oak, Holmbury St Mary

The Royal Oak is a compact cosy pub set back from the road below the church with a garden at the front. Now owned by Pubmaster this 17th century inn was once frequented by smugglers. At the other end of the social scale George II and Pitt the Elder were visitors in the 19th century. Young's ales are featured together with Green King IPA and Ansells Bitter.

Sandwiches and snacks are available and the blackboard menu that changes daily features homemade dishes like steak and ale pie, chicken curry, lasagne verdi and salmon fish cakes. The ham is home baked and the salads include avocado and prawn and roast beef.

There are two en-suite bedrooms.

Dogs are welcome but children are not allowed in the bar area.

Opening hours are 11am-3pm and 6-11pm, Sundays 12-3pm and 6-10.30pm.

Tel: 01306 730120.

Walk No. 26

The Royal Oak is situated in the centre of Holmbury St Mary by the church. On the B2126, it is reached by turning south off the A25 at Abinger Hammer 5 miles west of Dorking. There is parking at the pub.

Approx. distance of walk: 3½ miles. Start at OS Map Ref. TQ 110445.

The Royal Oak is close to point 3 of Walk 1 should you wish to combine the walks. Pick a clear day for this walk in the forest to get the full benefit from the views from Holmbury Hill, reached by a gentle ascent path on the Greensand Way.

1. Turn R out of the pub and R again on the drive beside the church. Follow the church boundary round to the L and enter a path along the top of the churchyard. Exit through a gate onto a hillside path behind gardens. Turn R on a lane and opposite the Kings Head fork R uphill. At a junction turn R and in 35 yards turn sharp R on a track signed for the cricket club. Bear L uphill and opposite the cricket pitch take the L fork, the Greensand Way (GW). At a junction of tracks on Somerset Hill turn L before a seat. At a waymarked fork go R on the GW. In June foxgloves and honeysuckle line the path. Ignore side paths to the R and at a fork go L, still on the GW, to the viewpoint and seat on top of Holmbury Hill. There is a toposcope to indicate the landmarks.

2. Leave the hill on the waymarked GW to the left of a Hurtwood Control collection box. Stay on the GW bearing L at several forks to reach a small lily pond on the R. Turn R passing the pond on your R. At a crossing path go half L for 10 yards, then bear R over a wide crossing track. Pass a Hurtwood Pinetum cairn on your L and go ahead on a wide track. Ignore side paths and at a major fork after ½ mile keep L. Just before a pond on the R cross a sleeper bridge and turn L up the side of the pond. A family of treecreepers entertained us here.

3. Turn R at the top of the pond and L at a fork passing a Millennium waymark post on your L. At the end of the Holmbury Youth Hostel car park (in 2002 there was talk of the hostel closing) turn R on a signed bridleway (The fingerpost is 30 yards to the L beside the car park). In 40 yards at a fork go L then R on a path under telegraph wires. At a telegraph pole with a yellow peril notice turn L and at a fork go R down to a wide track. Turn L then R on a crossing track uphill. Just over the top of a rise turn L on a path going steeply downhill. At a 'T' junction before gardens turn R and continue to a road, where turn R back to the pub.

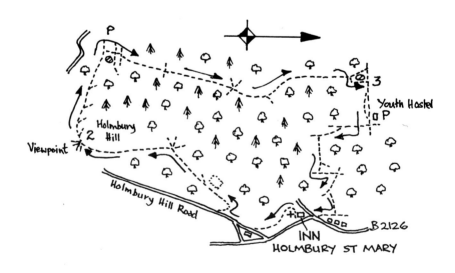

The Three Horseshoes, Irons Bottom

We felt instantly at home entering this welcoming little village local run by The Merry Wives of Sidlow (the next village). I suppose that an iron bottom might inhibit a wife's merriment but The Merry Wives of Iron Bottoms could have a certain ring to it. Pam and the other ladies seem to have got the formula just right. A free house, they offer Harvey's excellent Sussex bitter, Fullers ESB and London Pride and Youngs bitter, with Waggledance as a seasonal novelty.

The comprehensive snack menu has choices of ploughman's, baguettes, omelettes and 'Andy Capp' filled Yorkshire puddings. The usual pub main courses are available and there is a daily specials board all at very reasonable prices for Surrey and the cooking was excellent.

Dogs, other than guide dogs are not allowed and children in the garden only.

The pub has en-suite letting rooms and is open from 12-2.30pm weekdays, 12-3pm weekends and 5.30-11pm, 10.30pm Sunday.

Tel: 01293 862315.

Walk No. 27

Irons Bottom lies south of the A25 east of Dorking and is reached via Brockham and Leigh. At Leigh follow the sign for Charlwood for 1 mile then turn left for 1 mile and first left again. The pub is on the right and has ample parking space.

Approx. distance of walk: 5 miles. Start at OS Map Ref. TQ 249463.

A flat walk on lanes and fields in quiet countryside.

1. Cross the road from the pub to the telephone box and take the footpath across the field and turn L on a tree lined drive for ½ mile. A sparrowhawk watched our progress from a dead branch high on the R. At a waymark post before Bures Manor fork L round the garden and continue on a concrete drive. The concrete ends and the track bends R past a 3 fingered post. The concrete resumes and you go through a waymarked gate and past Bury's Court School over on the L. Just past a metal gate on the R cross a stile and join a faint path through fields with the R. Mole to your R. Cross a footbridge and continue to a stile where turn L on a road.

2. Opposite the postbox past Little Flanchford Cottages turn L on a path beside a field. Cross a stile and go diagonally R over the end of the field to a footbridge and stile, then turn sharp R to another stile and footbridge. Maintain direction along the RH side of 3 fields. On entering the fourth field fork diagonally L to a kissing gate at the bottom of the field. Turn L on a road and in 20 yards turn L through a kissing gate into Leigh churchyard. Pass to the L of the end of the church and at a 'T' junction turn L. Look R here for an old style 'bedboard' grave marker for a member of the Charrington Brewery family, summoned apparently to change the barrel in the bar upstairs. Follow the path out of the churchyard across a field and a footbridge and over a stile in a

hedge. Turn R down the field with the hedge on your R. Follow the hedge along the bottom of the field, cross a stile and turn L on a bridleway.

3. After 150 yards go through a waymarked gate and turn R along the field edge to a stile. Maintain direction diagonally across the next field to a stile in the corner. Continue along a fence beside a bluebell copse. Reach a stile on the L and turn R across the field to an Ordnance Survey trig. point pillar and enjoy the views. Now turn sharp L back to the corner of the field. (This really is the correct footpath from the OS Map). Cross a stile and head down the RH side of a field to another. Turn R beside the drive of Dene Farm to a waymarked field gate. Do not enter but cross the drive and bear half R across a field to a stile in the hedge then straight down the next field to a road.

4. Turn L past houses and L again on a drive signed to Stumblehole Farm. Admire the Poll Hereford pedigree herd and pass the farm, anything but a stumblehole, whatever that is. Just before Tamworth Farm on the R turn R over a stile to a path that crosses 2 fields via stiles. At the third stile bear diagonally R to a point about 15 yards above the field corner. Cross a sleeper bridge and a narrow field and turn R on the drive you started on. Cross the bridge and fork R on the footpath back to the pub.

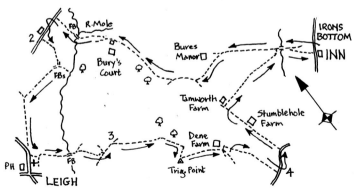

66

The Star, Lingfield

The big square Star with its car park at the front is not the 'chocolate box' thatched tavern you mght hope to find nestling in Old Lingfield. It is a spacious family pub where children are made particularly welcome, with a choice of eight meals including a drink and ice cream all at £2.95 in 2002. The garden has 2 play areas, one exclusive to the under fives, an aviary, 2 horses and 4 cats – say 'Hello' to Gigi for me. Dogs are allowed in the pub but not in the garden.

The ale selection on our visit was Everard's Tiger, Shepherd Neame Spitfire, Brains' Bitter and their own Star brewed by Flowers, with a choice of eight wines by the glass.

The menu includes sandwiches, jackets, burgers and tortilla wraps, nut roast and pub staples like steak and kidney pudding, ham, egg and chips, cod in beer batter, all day breakfast and fisherman's pie. The specials board changes daily.

The pub is open from 12-3pm and 5-11pm weekdays and all day weekends.

Tel: 01342 832364.

Walk No. 28

Lingfield can be reached by turning south off the M25 onto the A22 at junction 6. After Blindley Heath turn left on the B2029 (Ray Lane). In Lingfield turn left at the roundabout signed Edenbridge and left again into Church Road. The Star is on the right with a car park in front. Lingfield Station is on the route.

Approx. distance of walk: 5½ miles. Start at OS Map Ref. TQ 390437.

A walk over farmland and beside the Eden Brook. We came to Lingfield for the historic church and old village and a short stroll on the common. This walk is courtesy of a lady we met in the church who insisted that we must walk to Haxted Mill and drew the route on my maps with an orange highlighter pen. Thanks be to her.

1. Cross the road to the church past a photogenic group of mediaeval buildings. The church is a brass rubber's heaven and has many fascinating monuments and artefacts dating back to the 14th century. The Guide is money well spent. Continue through the churchyard and down steps past the library. Turn R back to Church Rd and cross into Bakers Lane. At a 'T' junction bear L to a white gate and cross the railway line. Continue on a track, bear L before Park Farm and join a signed footpath past houses, then on a grassy track. Cross a stile by a gate and immediately another on the L and turn R down the field edge with the hedge on your R. The thistles here were a magnet to goldfinches and numerous butterflies. At the end of the field go through a waymarked gate and bear R to a lone oak tree beside a sawn off stump. Here turn L to a gate at the bottom of the field.

2. Cross a lane and a stile and bear R on a (probably overgrown) path beside Eden Brook, another good site for birds and butterflies. Cross a stile and footbridge and bear half R to a stile in the bottom RH corner of the field. Turn R on a road for ½ mile to Haxted Mill. It is a delightful spot to stop for refreshments and the restored 15th century watermill houses a museum. 01732 862914 for opening hours. Retrace your steps from the mill to the near side of the bridge and turn L over a stile waymarked Vanguard Way. The R. Eden is to your R and you cross it by footbridge at the end of the field. Bear half L across a field to a stile and turn L on a road.

3. At a fork go R for ¼ mile then turn L over a stile at a fingerpost. Follow a defined path down a long field to a stile near the bottom RH corner. Maintain direction down the next field and bear R at the bottom to cross

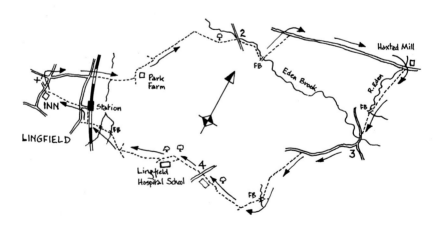

a footbridge. Keep to the LH edge of 2 fields then turn R along the end of the field, still with the hedge on your L. Continue along another field, turn R at the bottom and in 15 yards cross a footbridge onto a football field. Bear R along the touchline and on to the hedge at the end, where turn R to a gap and out to a road.

4. Turn L then in a few yards R over a stile. Cross 2 fields via stiles and enter woodland. Fork R by the gates of a play area. Just before the path leaves the woods, with a shed ahead, turn R through double metal gates. Continue along the LH edge of 2 fields. Half way down the second field bear L to join a more distinct path to a kissing gate and on over 2 footbridges and 2 fields to cross the railway line just south of Lingfield Station. Turn R up to the station then L on the road. At a 'T' junction cross to the footpath opposite and back to the pub.

Haxted Mill

Mediaeval Buildings, Lingfield

69

The Mariners, Millbridge

The Mariners is a smart hotel with 21 en-suite rooms, a bistro style restaurant decorated with fishing scenes and hung with fishing nets and an integral pub. It is a popular starting point for the many walks traversing Frensham Common. I liked everything about it, the Greene King Abbot, IPA and special Jubilation ale, the succulent pork chop and the general excitement as England beat Argentina 1-0 to round off a great week for Great Britain.

Amid the euphoria I also wrote down that the children enjoyed their mini pizzas and home made chicken goujons and the fresh fish, salads and turkey curry were all consumed with relish or even HP sauce. There are 13 pizza toppings and 21 country wines available.

Well behaved dogs are welcome in the bar and garden.

The Mariners is open all day every day and food is served all day from noon at weekends. Mon-Fri from 12-2pm and 6-9.45pm.

Tel: 01252 792050.

The Mariners is situated at Millbridge on the A287, 3 miles south of Farnham. There is parking at the hotel.

Approx. distance of walk: 5 miles but can be curtailed after 3 miles. Start at OS Map Ref. SU 848421.

A walk of interest to bird watchers over heathland, around a lake with reed beds and through woodland and gorse. We counted 28 species including Dartford warbler, reed warbler, stonechat, heron, redstart, linnet and sand martin.

1. Turn R out of the pub, cross the road and the R Wey and turn L on Priory Lane. Where the lane bends sharp L go ahead through a car park onto a wide track. At a major fork keep R and follow blue topped posts ignoring side paths. Just past post no. 520 turn L following orange arrows, soon to turn R over a boardwalk. Turn L at the end.

2. At a barrier by a Frensham Little Pond notice turn L on a path that skirts the pond. The reedbeds are to your L. At the end of the pond turn L beside a wall across an outlet to reach a road, where turn L. Pass a private road on the L and turn L to go between National Trust boards to the bank of the pond. Go over a crossing track by a 'keep dogs on leads' post and take the R fork ahead of you. Ignore turnings and follow orange arrows back to the car park. At this point you could turn L down Priory Lane back to The Mariners.

3. If you want more, turn sharp L by a blue post in the car park onto a footpath into woodland. At a fork keep R then over a crossing path past a barrier. At a 'T' junction and barrier turn L passing houses on the R. The track bends R and at a 'T' junction by post no.43 turn R. At a fork keep R and cross the A287. Follow orange arrows to reach a junction with fine views L over Frensham Great Pond. Go R here past post no. 45 then fork L following a yellow arrow. Go over a wide grass track and onto a path through gorse downhill to a road.

4. Turn L and in 25 yards turn R at a fingerpost. Follow this narrow path to cross one road and reach another, where turn L then R before St Mary the Virgin Church. Cross the R. Wey by the Old Malt House and in 15 yards at a waymark fork R through a gate, then another gate. Cross a footbridge and at a fork keep L uphill to a 'T' junction where turn R. Fork L to a signpost and turn R with a fence on your L. Cross a stile and continue down hill to emerge beside the pub.

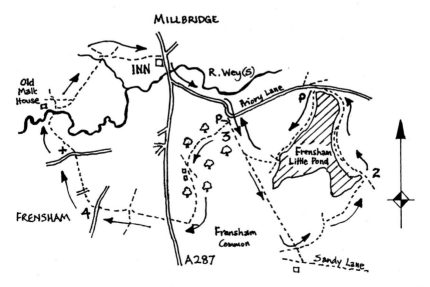

The Six Bells, Newdigate

The Six Bells is an attractive 2 bar local with an inglenook fireplace. To the rear is a restaurant area, patio and beer garden. The pub enjoys an elevated position opposite the picturesque church and watching the weddings is a popular Saturday diversion. The bridegrooms and supporters come to quaff pre-nuptial Dutch courage or, to be accurate, English Tanglefoot, Badger or Sussex ale. The bride takes an eternity to exit the Rolls and adjust her finery. Then it all goes quiet for ½ hour before the pub fills up again with a herd of male escapees toasting yet another near miss. On the Sunday many will return to consult the infamous Ephraim Knoller who has an interesting line in hangover cures. On our visit the pub had just been acquired by Hall and Woodhouse, the decorators were sprucing up the exterior and the menu had received a much needed make over.

Snacks include sandwiches, ploughman's and jackets. The blackboard menu is headed by ½ honey roast duck with Hawaiian chicken, steak and kidney pudding, steak and ale pie, vegetable stir fry, fresh trout, grilled sea bass, etc. There is also a children's selection.

Dogs are welcome.

Opening hours are Mon-Sat 11am-3pm and 6-11pm. Sun 12-3pm and 6-10.30pm.

Tel: 01306 631276.

Newdigate is about 5 miles south of Dorking. Take the A24 and after 1 mile turn left signed Blackbrook and follow the road through to Newdigate. The Six Bells is opposite the church and there is a car park at the pub.

Approx. distance of walk: 5 miles. Start at OS Map Ref. TQ 197420. The walk may be combined with Walk 11 at Point 3.

A flat walk over farmland and through woods passing 4 pretty ponds and plenty of bird life.

1. Cross the road from the pub into Church Lane. Just past George Horley Place turn R over a stile and cross the field to a stile in the bottom LH corner. Turn R past a shed and cross a field to a telegraph pole then on through a gate. Continue with a hedge on your L, cross a footbridge and maintain direction to a gate. Bear half L across the next field to a stile. Go over a crossing track to join a track between fields and turn R before a waymarked gate. Cross a footbridge between 2 fishponds resplendent with pink water lilies in August. Geese and herons are usually here when the anglers are absent. Bear half R to the far corner of the field – this is rarely walked and there is no path. Cross a stile and go forward a few yards to turn L on a path. Look out for kestrels over the fields and yellow hammers in the hedgerows. Go through a small metal gate, then another and turn L on a farm road.

2. Fork L immediately onto a wide grass track that soon bends L. Go through a gateway and between private ponds with white waterlilies, then past a bluebell wood on the R, part of a nature reserve. Continue for

another ½ mile, turn R on Partridge Lane then L into Charlwood Lane. Just past the 40mph sign turn L on a signed bridleway lined with bluebells in season.

3. Just before 2 waymark posts (Point 3 on Walk 11) turn L over a sleeper bridge to a path between fields. Turn R on a road then, in a few yards, turn L on a footpath. Cross a stile and advance to a telegraph pole in the middle of the field, then turn R to a way-marked stile. Maintain direction with a hedge on your L through a field opening. At the hedge corner turn L and follow it down to the copse at the bottom, again there is no discernible path. Turn R before the trees and follow the field edge. At the end turn L through the trees to a stile and gate. Join a path, go through a gate, pass Copse View and continue on a track past a waymarked telegraph pole. Turn L on Cudworth Lane past the moated Cudworth Manor. At a 'T' junction turn R. A deer sitting under the apple trees in the Orchard was happy to stare us out – perhaps they are cider apples? Turn L on Church Lane and back to the pub.

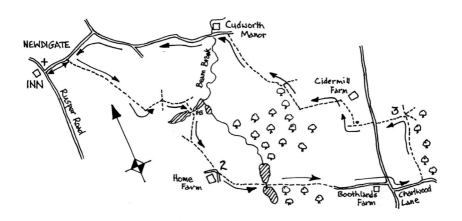

73

The Cricketers' Arms, Ockley

The Cricketers' Arms was originally an ale house on Roman Stane Street before that became the A29 racetrack to the coast. The pub retains an authentic old world charm with exposed beams, horse brasses, flagstone floors and an inglenook fireplace. The patio at the front is outstanding, featuring hibiscus and dahlias of show standard and there is a garden with fishpond to the side.

The ales are the excellent Ringwood Bitter and London Pride.

Even on Sundays when there is a choice of 4 roast lunches, there is a comprehensive menu of sandwiches, plain and toasted, 5 ploughmans and 7 salads, vegetarian lasagne, chilli and korma, and pub staple dishes like fish and chips, ham or sausage egg and chips etc. The roast was home cooking at its best.

Children are welcome and dogs on leads.

Opening hours are 11am-3pm and 6-11pm, Sunday open all day from 12 noon. Food is served until 2.15pm.

Tel: 01306 627205.

The Cricketers' Arms at Ockley is 6 miles south of Dorking on the A29 just south of the village green. There is parking behind the pub. The walk passes close to Ockley and Capel Station and may be joined from there at Point 2 – see map.

Approx. distance of walk: 4½ miles. Start at OS Map Ref. TQ 145397.

A favourite walk starting on an attractive village green then going through blue-bell woods and over farmland with a visit to a nature reserve and lake. As is inevitably the case we saw nothing of interest in the nature reserve but plenty of wildlife elsewhere. There may be mud in the woods.

1. Turn L out of the pub and L on the track around the village green where there is some interesting old property and a nice view of Leith Hill and Tower to the L. Pass the lily pond with resident Egyptian Geese and turn R to cross the A29 and take the signed footpath next to the Post Office. Cross a stile and maintain direction up a field and over 2 more stiles. Turn R to a stile by a gate but do not cross it. Turn L along the field edge to a gate leading to a bridleway through a bluebell wood. Look out for deer here. Cross a footbridge and go uphill and over a waymarked crossing path now beside a field. Bear L round a garden and continue to a road.

2. Turn R on Weare St for 700 yards then turn R on Vann Lake Rd. The telegraph wires here are a swallow and house martin gathering place and there must have been 200 or more when we passed in late August. Where Vann Lake Rd turns R keep ahead. The road becomes a track and in 20 yards turn R down steps by a Nature Reserve notice. Bear L along the lakeside path past the boathouse. At the end of the lake you can explore further but to continue the walk turn L back to the track then turn R.

3. Opposite the second shed in the garden of Rill Cottage turn L between posts and bear L past a pond to join a bridleway into woods. Go over a crossing track, then a second and

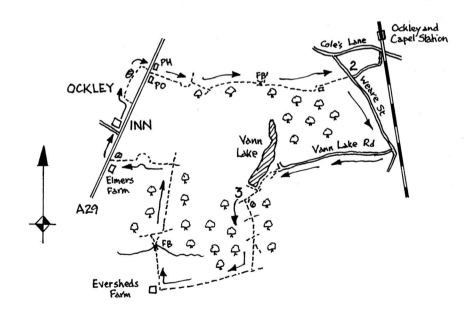

75

fork R before a bridleway marker post. At a 'T' junction before a field turn R to a field entrance. Maintain direction up a field towards farm buildings. Dozens of young pheasants scattered from the hedge on the L as we passed. Just before the first barn turn R over a stile and head up the LH side of a field to a stile into woods. Go downhill to cross a footbridge and immediately fork L up to a wide crossing track where turn R. In 75 yards turn L before a new plantation. Stay on this track ignoring side turnings to reach a gate. Continue up a field to a stile on the R where turn L across the field to another stile. Go forward to a hedge corner then turn R and follow the hedge round to the L and then R and on down the drive of Elmers Farm. Turn R on the A29 back to the pub.

Village Pond, Ockley

Vann Lake, Ockley

The Ram's Nest Inn, Ramsnest Common

The quaintly named Ram's Nest was built as a pub in 1796 by two men who allegedly murdered their employer and used his money for that purpose, possibly burying the body in the foundations. Now somewhat isolated on the A283 Petworth Road between Chiddingfold and Northchapel, it deserves to have a thriving community to serve. I liked everything about it, the welcome, the cosy atmosphere, the sensible separation of the TV and pool table, the wishing well and the eccentric garden statuary.

A Greene King house, Abbot and IPA are available with Hogs Back TEA. There is a snack menu and a mouth watering blackboard featuring such as homemade onion and celery soup, stir fried duck breast, smoked chicken and avocado salad, homemade steak and ale pie, pan fried guinea fowl and seafood platter. The garden has a play area and dogs are also welcome.

There are two en-suite letting rooms.

Opening hours are Mon-Fri 11am-3pm and 6-11pm. Sat 11am-11pm and Sun 12-10.30pm.

Tel: 01428 644460.

Walk No. 32

The Ram's Nest Inn is situated at Ramsnest Common 2 miles south of Chiddingfold on the A283 Petworth Road. There is parking at the pub.

Approx. distance of walk: 4½ miles. Start at OS map Ref. SU 949329.

A walk on lanes and farmland through bluebell woods and along the Sussex Border Path. The Walk may be combined with Walk 12 at Point 2.

1.   Turn R out of the pub and R into Gostrode Lane. Just past Gostrode farm-house fork R beside a pond, go through a gate and ahead on a signed bridleway, then through a waymarked gate and beside a fence with a bluebell wood to the L. Turn R over a waymarked stile and bear half L up a meadow keeping to the R of oak trees. Cross a stile into a large field (full of 5ft. high broad beans in June 2002). Go ahead then the path curves gently L down to a stile into a meadow. Pass to the L of a fenced copse and out to a road. Turn L for 500 yds and just before Corry Mead turn R over a stile into a meadow. (Point 3 of Walk 12 is a little further up the road.)

2.   Cross a meadow to a stile on the R and continue over 2 more fields and stiles then with a fence to your R for 2 fields. Finally go through a hedge via stiles and bear half L to a gate and a road. In Feb 2002 there was a proposal to close the path through Robins Farm leading to the Sussex Border Path. So,

just in case, turn R here and L at a 'T' junction signed Shillinglee. Look for a gate on the L and cross the top of a field to a path uphill into a bluebell wood. Cross a stile by a gate on the R into a farmyard. Go to the L of a metal gate and out to the road via way-marked gates.

3.   Cross the road and continue on the Sussex Border Path keeping to the LH edge of 4 fields. A fine dog fox sauntered down the path ahead of us and yellowhammers on the hedge top bemoaned the scarcity of cheese. Ignore the small wooden gate on the L and eventually go through a gate into a copse and downhill over a crossing path. Emerge via a gate and continue along the LH side of a field with a bluebell wood to the L. Opposite a stile on the L go half R across a field to cross a stile. Keep beside the fence on the L to reach a stile by a shed and out to Gostrode Lane, where turn L back to the pub.

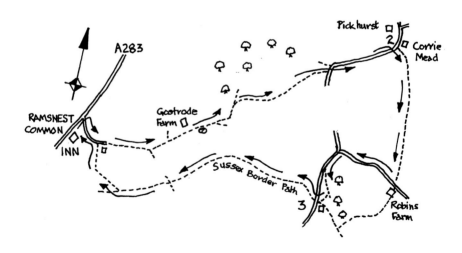

The Sea Horse, Shalford

The Sea Horse is a Vintage Inn offering that group's standard décor, menu, wine list and Bass and Tetley ales. The pub is nicely laid out with a central bar and several dining areas and the service is efficient and attentive.

Selections from the menu include tortilla wrap and brown bloomer sandwiches, 'smaller plates' such as salmon and broccoli fishcakes and main courses like beef Wellington, lemon chicken, gammon steak or baked sea bass. A notice warns that 'this is an over 21 pub'. While we were there a couple of 'over 21' midgets in frilly knickers and bare feet were running all over the place but it might be as well to check before arriving with a gang of teenagers. Just before going to press I heard that The Sea Horse had won the Mayor's prize as Guildford 'Pub of the Year' 2002. The wine list and service are above average but I have been in six Vintage Inn pubs and they are all virtually identical and the managers have no freedom to vary the menu or to introduce guest ales. In such circumstances I wonder how they can be conceivably rated above some of the excellent free houses within Guildford Borough. See what you think.

Dogs in the garden area only.

Opening hours are 11am-11pm Monday to Saturday and 12-10.30pm Sundays. Tel: 01483 514351.

Walk No. 33

The Sea Horse is situated in The Street, Shalford, part of the A281, one mile south of Guildford. There is parking at the pub. Shalford Station is about 500 yards south of the pub.

Approx. distance of walk: 5½ miles. Start at OS Map Ref. TQ 001476.

The walk could be combined with Walk 9 at Point 2 and Walk 13 at Point 4. Coming from Guildford Station (approx 550 yards) the walk could be joined in Quarry St., where turn L past the Museum into Castle St and follow Para 3. This walk starts along a delightful stretch of the R. Wey, visits a ruined castle and goes on up to the N. Downs with fine views. The return is through woodland and across fields with abundant wildflowers and birdsong in summer.

1. Turn L out of the pub and L again beyond the car park onto a bridleway. At a fork advance to a gate and turn L on the path above the track. At a 'T' junction turn R through a kissing gate, down to a metal gate and on to cross a board walk. Turn L along the riverbank, cross a weir and turn L along the bank. Cross another weir and continue along the bank of the R. Wey Navigation.

2. Cross over at St Catherine's Lock (Point 4 on Walk 9) and turn R along the towpath for ½ mile. At a fork before a picnic area cross a footbridge and keep R to another that leads out to the A281. Turn L, cross the road at the traffic lights and turn L up Quarry Street.

3. Turn R into Castle St. In the castle grounds to the L is a statue of Alice Through the Looking Glass commemorating Charles Dodgson (Lewis Carroll). Continue up Castle Hill and turn L at the top. Look out L for a fine view of Guildford Cathedral before turning R up Pewley Hill. When the road ends continue on the bridleway to the trig. point. On Pewley Down give thanks for the Friary Brewery. Just beyond the trig. point bear R downhill with a hedge on your L. At a 'T' junction with a waymark post to your L turn R downhill between hedges. Skylarks, whitethroats and wrens may compete for your attention here. Go over a crossing track by a Pewley Down

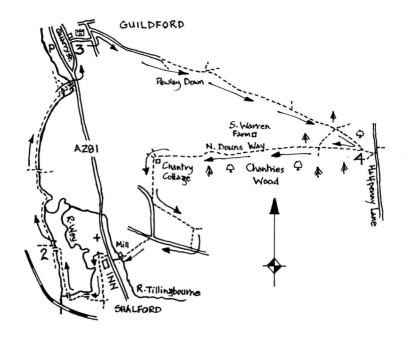

80

notice and join the footpath on the L above the horse path.

4. Where the footpath rejoins the bridleway at a junction if you want to combine with Walk 13 go forward to Halfpenny Lane. Otherwise turn sharp R downhill on the N. Downs Way. Go over a crossing track and pass South Warren Farm. On reaching Chantry Cottage turn L on a path with a fence on your R. At a road turn L and in 25 yards at a double fingerpost turn sharp L past a stile. In June 2002 this field had not been treated with weed killer and among the rape were hosts of red poppies, white ox-eye daisies and blue Venus's looking glass. With a skylark singing overhead it was a Jubilee celebration fit for a Queen. At a waymark post in the middle of the field turn R then R over a stile onto a lane. Opposite a side road turn up steps on the L, cross a stile and turn R across a field to another stile. Go down steps past the National Trust owned Shalford Mill standing over the R. Tillingbourne. The pub is directly opposite the end of the lane.

Shalford Mill

River Wey, Shalford

The Red Lion, Shamley Green

The Red Lion has a cosy bar and a larger restaurant and there are gardens front and rear.

Ales on offer were Adnams Broadside, Tetley's Imperial and Young's bitter and a choice of wines by the glass.

The extensive menu offers sandwiches plain and toasted, New Zealand green lip mussels, giant prawns in garlic butter, lasagne al forno, mixed fish and prawn pie, half crispy roast duck and many more. All the food coming out of the kitchen looked better than the average pub grub and the salads in June 2002 were quite the best we have seen in a pub judged on quality, variety of ingredients, presentation and value for money.

The pub has some letting rooms and is open all day every day with lunches served from 12-3pm.

Children are welcome but dogs in the garden only, please.

Tel: 01483 892202.

The Red Lion is situated at Shamley Green on the B2128 between Guildford and Cranleigh. There is parking at the pub or at the roadside.

Approx. distance of walk: 4 miles. Start at OS Map Ref. TQ 033438.

A varied walk over farmland where skylarks sing along a section of the Greensand Way, rising through bluebell woods for fine views and a herd of deer. Mud and nettles may be hazards in Section 3.

1. Turn L out of the pub then first R beside the green, later joining Hullbrook Lane. At a 'T' junction go R then in 25 yards L on a bridleway soon between fields. At a 'T' junction bear L and cross the R. Wey. Just before an arch turn up L to a disused railway track and turn L.

2. Just before another arch turn up R then L to cross the bridge. At a fork go R through a gate waymarked Greensand Way (GW). Maintain direction across a meadow, a footbridge and through 2 gates. Fork R at a waymark post, cross a drive and through a gate. Cross a farm track and follow GW signs across a road and onto a path to the R of Shamley Green Church. Pucker up for 3 kissing gates and at a 'T' junction go R. Maintain direction on a drive that bends L to a road.

3. Turn L and in 25 yards R on a bridleway uphill. At a 'T' junction turn R and at the next junction before a barn turn L. At a fingerpost turn L on a path and look L for deer. Beware nettles and rabbit holes as you descend to cross 2 stiles, a field and 2 more stiles then bear L. At a road turn R and at a fork R again past the pond and back to the pub.

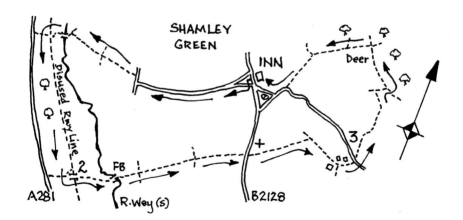

The Prince of Wales, Shere

Shere is blessed with two pubs. If any of your party are fractious you can deposit them in the stocks outside the White Horse while you enjoy the Prince of Wales Free House. On a sunny Sunday in May the garden and bars were packed with diners.

From a most impressive menu roast beef and lamb were popular. But a perfect grilled sea bass and fresh dressed crab salad still reached the table before I had consumed one pint of Shepherd Neame's Spitfire. Impressive cooking and efficient cheery service under pressure. Also on offer were London Pride and Young's Bitter, and a choice of 12 wines by the glass. The "little extras" were remarkable, for example, a choice of six mustards and some seriously sinful puddings such as brandy snap baskets filled with orange and Cointreau ice cream. There is a children's menu and they can also have smaller portions of some main courses.

Opening hours are weekdays 11am-3pm and 5-11pm; weekends all day. The pub is (clean) dog friendly.

Tel: 01483 202313.

Shere is situated just south of the A25 between Guildford and Dorking. The Prince of Wales is in Shere Lane in the centre of the village. There is parking behind the pub.

Approx. distance of walk: 6 miles (3½ + 2½). Start at OS Map Ref. TQ 072478.

They say Shere is so nice you will want to go there twice. Certainly this pretty village warrants a full day's attention. The walk is designed to give morning exercise taking the direct route up to the N Downs Way and back via the Silent Pool and Silver Wood. Then there is the option of an afternoon stroll south of the village with time to wander and visit the 12th century church and museum. Guide booklets are available.

1. Turn L out of the pub and over the river bridge. At a 'T' junction turn L and in 25 yards R up a track beside a sports field. Pass under the A25 and trudge uphill to reach a circular concrete reservoir. Turn L here signed N. Downs Way. Pass through Hollister Farm and follow the lane round to the R, then take the second fork on the L. Turn L on a road then R up Staple Lane to West Hanger car park.

2. Turn L signed N Downs Way for ½ mile, then turn L signed Silent Pool. Half way along a field on the R turn L on a narrow path then down steps to the Silent Pool. Bear R along the water's edge and be sure to read the legend at the kiosk. Continue past the second pond and at a lane turn L past Sherbourne Farm that is often open to visitors.

3. Turn L at the A25, cross over and turn R on the path beside the A248. At a fingerpost by a Victorian post box turn L to cross a stile and then a field. Maintain direction trough Silver Wood, where you should see pheasants and bluebells in season, exit via a gate and cross a pasture to a kissing gate. Cross a lane to a path beside a wall then turn R on a road. Cross a footbridge over the R Tillingbourne by a ford and turn L beside the river then R back to the pub.

4. For the second circuit cross to the Church of St James. Opposite the end of the church take the path to the R uphill between fences, go through a gate and over a crossing track. Continue up the field with a fence on your R, through a gate and over a railway footbridge. Keep ahead with a fence on your R then turn R at a waymark now with a wall to

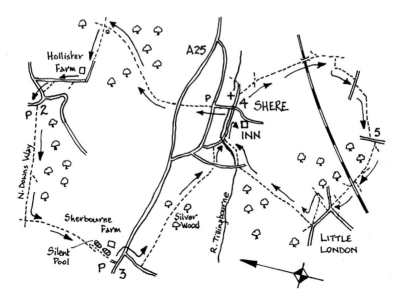

your L. At a 'T' junction turn L uphill past houses and enjoy the view to the R. At a road turn R and in a few yards L at a finger-post. Keep beside the fence on the R to join a path between fences.

5. Cross a stile and then a road into woodland. Ignore the L fork in a few yards and pass Albury Borehole No.4. Join a lane and pass cottages. As it bends L go forward to white gates and re cross the railway. At an immediate fork keep ahead, go over a crossing track and reach a road junction. Cross the road and turn R on a signed bridleway into woods. At the second waymark post turn sharp L and at a road turn sharp R through a kissing gate to pass some magnificent chestnut trees. One artistic observer likened the lower bark to 'swirling skirts'. There is a bluebell wood over to the R, a picture in early May. Go through a kissing gate and beside the Tillingbourne. Leave the meadow through another kissing gate and maintain direction on a track to the ford and on as before back to the pub.

Church of St. James, Shere

The Volunteer, Sutton Abinger

The handsome, welcoming Volunteer, originally converted from four worker's cottages and dating from 1630 has been a favourite pub since we joined their VE Day jubilee celebrations in 1995. The raised garden always offers a fine view and that night it was enhanced by a jazz band and a fireworks display. The Olde Worlde bars and open fire are popular with walkers particularly in winter.

Taken over by Hall and Woodhouse in 1998 it has gone upmarket and now displays endorsements from The Good Pub Guide, Les Routiers and cheese and seafood promoters. Tanglefoot, Badger and Sussex bitter are available and 9 wines by the glass.

Seafood featured includes lobster, crab and seabass and the cod is in Tanglefoot batter. Other offerings include Moroccan lamb tagine, Weiner schnitzel, five cheese quiche, green Thai curry and smoked mackerel salad. The ploughman's comes with homemade bread.

Children and dogs are welcome and opening hours are Mon-Fri 12-2.30pm and 6-11pm. Weekends open all day.

Tel: 01306 730798

Walk No. 36

The Volunteer can be reached by turning south off the A25 at Abinger Hammer onto the B2126 for about 1½ miles then take the first turning left. There is parking at the pub.

Approx. distance of walk: 5 miles. Start at OS Map Ref. TQ 105459.

A walk commencing on farmland were skylarks sing and partridges whirr overhead, passing a lovely pond and some watercress beds before tackling the lower slopes of the North Downs. There are fine views and the return is through Abinger Hammer and across farmland. Walk 1 passes The Volunteer so the two can be combined.

1.Turn L out of the pub into Raikes Lane and in 50 yards turn L on a bridleway. Fork R at a gate and soon follow a field edge. At a fingerpost turn L and follow this path with fine views ahead to bear L then R through Paddington Farm. Swifts nest in the farmhouse eaves. Pass between a lovely pond and watercress beds and Paddington Mill.

2. Cross the A25 and head uphill. Follow a waymark past a gate and along a field edge, through a gate and into woods. At a waymarked 'T' junction turn R on a wide track then in 35 yards fork L on a grass track, passing between a waymark post and a seat. Fork R, soon downhill and over a crossing path, then turn R on a wide track to cross a railway bridge. Pass a farm and at a 'T' junction turn L. At the next waymarked 'T' junction turn L downhill. Ignore R turns and the path narrows between fields to re cross the railway. Pass Hackhurst Farm and

at a fingerpost turn R through a gate and along a field edge. Cross a stile into woods and at a fork keep ahead to a lane where turn L down to the A25.

3. Cross the road and turn L then R at a signed bridleway. Cross a footbridge and at a waymark post take the first path on the L uphill through a tunnel of arching trees. Turn L at a stile, then R along the field edge. At a fingerpost turn L across a field keeping to the R of trees. Cross a stile and bear R beside a fence, then L downhill. Cross a road and a stile, ignore a stile on the R and go ahead over the next stile. At the next fingerpost bear L across a field. Turn R along the hedge and at a telegraph pole bear L and turn R on the path you started out on. At a fingerpost keep ahead following yellow waymarks across 2 fields to reach Raikes Lane, where turn R back to the pub.

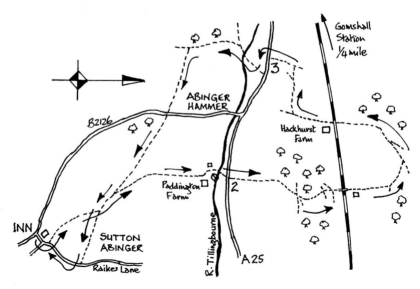

The Barley Mow, Tandridge

The Barley Mow is a handsome Hall and Woodhouse pub with a front patio and a beer garden at the rear. The recently refurbished interior has separate bar and restaurant areas. As expected the ales are Tanglefoot, Badger and Sussex Bitter with the added refinement of Sussex Mild.

Children are catered for with a choice of 5 dishes. The main menu is comprehensive with interesting entries like spinach and red pepper lasagne, steak and Tanglefoot pie, mushroom tortellini, chicken ham and leek pie, Brie and broccoli en croute and chicken fusilli along with staples like gammon, egg and chips and cod in beer batter. Dogs are welcome in the bar and garden and should be spruced up to meet Montgomery of Wessex an aristocratic Springer Spaniel.

The pub is open daily from 12 noon to 3pm and 5pm to 11pm (Sunday 10.30pm), with food served until 2pm.

Tel : 01883 713770.

Walk No. 37

The Barley Mow is in the centre of Tandridge in Tandridge Lane. From the A25 junction with the A22 turn east for ½ mile and take the second turning on the right for ½ mile. There is ample parking at the pub.

Approx. distance of walk: 4½ miles. Start at OS Map Ref. TQ 373507.

A walk starting along the Greensand Way over farmland and visiting a children's farm and playground at Godstone. The return passes ponds and a church restored by Sir George Gilbert Scott, who lived locally. Bridleways may be muddy.

1. Turn R out of the pub and in 25 yards turn L on the signed Greensand Way (GW). Don't worry about the stile going nowhere, the GW is the wide track through the fields down a dip and up to the A22. Cross over and maintain direction, still on the GW. At a fingerpost keep ahead with a pond on the L. Keep ahead at the next fingerpost, now with Leigh Place Pond to your R, and cross a footbridge. Continue on a drive to a road and turn R. Pass Church Lane and take the next turning L.
2. After 100 yards turn R on a signed footpath that climbs through woodland. Cross a stile to a fenced path into Godstone Farm. There is a right of way through the farm but if you want to stay there is an admission charge. Tel : 01883 742546. Follow the waymarks past the playground and pigsties and down to the entrance. 20 yards before the entrance kiosk turn R then immediately L on a path through a small gate and down to a road. Turn R and just past the 30mph signs turn L on a signed footpath beside fields. At The Barn turn R on a road for 250 yards to Godstone village green. Turn R

across the green to pass the pond and take the path to the R of the White Hart pub signed Parish Church. Bay Pond to the L, now a nature reserve with a good population of mallard and Canada Geese, was originally the power source for a gunpowder factory.
3. Cross a road into the churchyard and pass to the R of the church and out to a path. Pass a lily pond on your L and the path winds round to a waymark post at a field entrance. Turn R down the field edge then bear R to a stile and turn L on a signed bridleway that runs under the A22. Turn R before Hop Garden Cottage and follow the bridleway for ½ mile to a road. Turn R and at a 'T' junction turn L up to Tandridge Church standing next to a magnificent yew tree. Retrace your steps from the church and turn L on a drive signed Tandridge Farm Shop. Pass the farm and continue down the track. Just past a metal gate turn R through a waymarked kissing gate onto the GW and turn R up the field to a stile onto a path. Continue when this widens to a drive and leads you back to the pub.

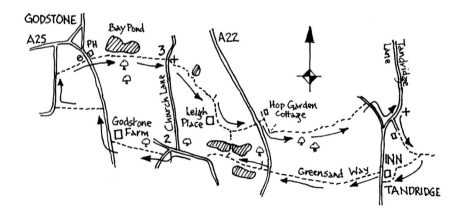

The Barley Mow, Tilford

Originally a pair of 18th century cottages until converted into an ale house, the Barley Mow, beside the much photographed Tilford Green, is always an attractive village pub. Decked out in Union Jacks and England flags for the Jubilee and World Cup it was a picture. The ales are Abbot, London Pride and Brakspears and Courage bitters.

The food selection has something for everyone; ploughmans, baps, toasted sandwiches, five salads, pork chop, steaks, stuffed aubergine, chicken and spinach curry are a few examples. There is a children's menu of smaller portions and a family room in the garden.

Dogs under control are welcome inside and out. Mobile phones are not - there is a £1 fine for charity if yours rings in the pub. The only drawback with the pleasant riverside garden is that you cannot watch the cricket from there.

Opening hours are weekdays 11-3pm and 6-11pm; weekends open all day. You would be wise to book at weekends.

Tel: 01252 792205.

Walk No. 38

The Barley Mow is reached via Tilford Street running south from the B3001 between Farnham and Elstead. Parking is beside the River Wey or at the roadside.

Approx. distance of walk: 4½ miles. Start at OS Map Ref. SU 873435.

A walk mainly over typical Surrey heath land with a chance of seeing nightjars and Dartford warblers, returning on bridle paths and beside the R.Wey. The latter section may be muddy.

1. Turn left out of the pub to view the mediaeval bridge over the R.Wey, then turn R past the car park and continue to a 'T' junction. Turn L onto a permissive bridle path (closed in January). Exit through a gate and turn L on a track. Pass Stockbridge Pond on the R, then a military barrier. At a junction of 3 paths take the one on the R in a gully. Fork R at a waymark post. Go over a crossing track and ahead up Yagden Hill. Horses ahead flushed a nightjar here.
2. At the next junction keep ahead on a path that bears R beside a golf course. Keep on this path with the golf course to your R for ½ mile. Go over a waymarked crossing path and at a 'T' junction turn R on a wide sandy track. At a fork go R and maintain direction passing the 14th tee on your L and out to a road.
3. Cross into Grange Road and continue for nearly ½ mile. Just past Spring Cottage on the R turn R on a signed bridleway. A fox ambled along in front of us past a wood yard. Keep ahead through nursery land and at a 'T' junction turn R on a Byway. In 150 yards turn left over a stile into woodland. After passing houses on the L fork L on a narrow path that leads beside the R.Wey South as it heads towards the confluence with the R.Wey North. There are bluebells here and in early summer masses of campions, ragged robin and other wild flowers. Continue past a gate onto an enclosed path to another gate to see the Barley Mow ahead across the green.

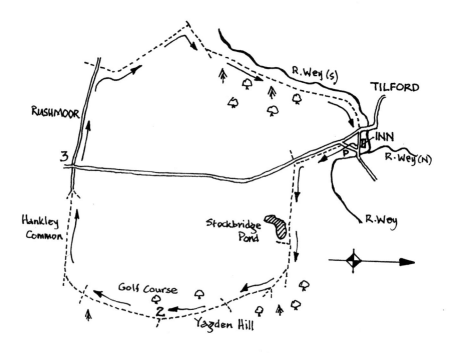

The White Hart, Witley

The White Hart has more class than most main road pubs. Dating from the 16th century the pub is thought to have the longest continually running licence in England and the original inn sign is now in the Victoria and Albert Museum. Two ghosts, one of each sex, are said to make their presence felt from time to time. On our visit the public bar had no such spirits and no barman either. The saloon was full so we were fortunate to be directed to the restaurant area where a tasteful jazz compilation tape enhanced the enjoyment of a generous ham ploughman's and a pint of Shepherd Neame's Spitfire with a Master Brew chaser.

Tasty pub grub and a separate children's menu including pizza were the lunchtime offerings and the restaurant evening menu was mouth watering. A pub with a nice atmosphere and pleasant welcoming staff.

Opening hours are 11am-3pm and 5.30-11pm weekdays and all day weekends. Tel: 01428 683695.

Walk No. 39

The White Hart is situated on the A283 Petworth road at the southern end of Witley. There is parking at the pub.

Approx. distance of walk: 4 miles. Start at OS Map Ref. SU 947397. Witley Railway Station is on the route.

A varied walk on country lanes and through wild flower meadows and woods passing pretty ponds and interesting buildings. This walk could be combined with Walk 23 to make a longer ramble.

1. Turn R out of the pub and R again at a fingerpost before Lashams. Go through a wooden gate on the L and across a meadow and out through a gate. Turn R past the wisteria clad Enton Mill and the millpond with resident geese and muscovy ducks. Continue under a railway bridge, pass some nice barn conversions and at a 'T' junction turn R. At the next 'T' junction cross to a narrow path going uphill. Cross a stile and follow a waymark across a meadow beautifully garnished with blue speedwell and golden buttercups in late May. Maintain direction, go through a kissing gate and cross a track to a grass path. In 20 yards you join the path common to Walk 23 if you want to combine the two.

2. Continue up the meadow with Enton Hall on your R passing the pond on your L. Go through a gate and at a fork go R on the narrower path. Look out for tree creepers here. Go over a crossing track and at a 'T' junction turn R. In a few yards fork L passing a house on the R to follow the waymarked bridleway uphill. At a fork follow the way-mark L and at a junction of paths by Moor Cottage turn R. Reach a road and turn R down to the A283.

3. Cross and turn L and in a few yards, before Little Gables, turn R onto a path to Witley railway station, confusingly situated in Wormley. Just past the Woodpigeon pub turn sharp R to the corner of the station car park. Join a narrow path and turn L to cross the railway footbridge. Continue on a path to cross a lane onto a dirt road. Pass a house on the R and at a road cross to a Greensand Way waymark then turn R onto a 'permissive footpath' going steeply uphill. At a 'T' junction turn R.

4. At a road cross to a bridleway by Woodbury Cottage. Continue on this path through woodland for ½ mile ignoring all paths off to the R. The path rises via steps to a road where turn R. Just past Hangerfield fork R onto a footpath beside the road. After ½ mile rejoin the road going down hill past All Saints church back to the pub.

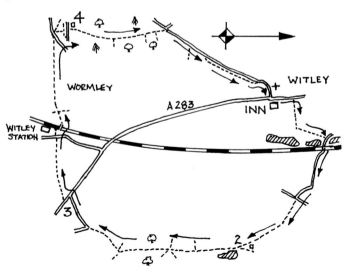

The Wotton Hatch, Wotton

The Wotton Hatch has been acquired by Vintage Inns and the new inn sign indicates their awareness of the walking heritage hereabouts. The décor is standard with several comfortable dining areas around a central bar. The garden is large and nicely laid out.

The beer is Tetley and Bass and there is a good choice of wines by the glass.

Snacks include chicken BLT with bloomer bread and chips and toasted ciabatta with tuna mayonnaise, roasted vegetables and melted mozzarella. The VI summer menu includes poached salmon salad, rump, pepper and gammon steaks, asparagus risotto, baked whole sea bass and chicken, leek and ham pie.

Dogs on leads are welcome. Well behaved children may be let off their leads at the owner's discretion.

The pub is open all day everyday with food served until 10pm.

Tel: 01306 732931.

Walk No. 40

Wotton Hatch is on the south side of the A25 about 2½ miles west of Dorking. The pub has a large car park.

Approx. distance of walk: 4½ miles. Start at OS Map Ref TQ 126475.

A walk on the Wotton Estate along the Tillingbourne valley and the Greensand Way through woods and farmland and a valley where linnets sing, finally visiting a church with fine views of the N.Downs. Section 2 is the same as Section 2 of Walk 20 should you wish to combine the walks.

1. Leave the back of the pub car park over a stile beside the Village Hall. Bear R across the field to a point about two thirds of the way down the fence and cross a stile onto the drive to Wotton House. The bank to the R is a mass of bluebells in season. At a finger-post turn L across a field and over the river and at a 'T' junction turn R. Soon the Tillingbourne runs in a succession of ponds below. Cross a stile by a bridge and turn L over another stile steeply uphill. Pass a gate on the L and keep beside the fence. Were the track bends L turn R at the bottom of a dip. This is point 2 on Walk 20.

2. Go ahead to cross a lane via kissing gates then beside a fence and downhill. Bear L to a stile and across a meadow and the river.

3. At a stile turn L on a track and away from Walk 20. At a fork past a fishpond turn R over a waymarked Greensand Way (GW) stile. Go uphill to a stile, turn L then L again at an immediate 'T' junction. Pause only to admire the view at a fingerpost, then continue and keep L where the track divides and runs parallel. Just before a metal gate

turn R over a stile (GW) into woods. The path swings L down to a stile and you maintain direction past houses and a magnificent redwood tree. Bear R on a road through The Rookery past the thatched Mill House and waterfall.

4. Turn L on the A25 and take the second turning R, Coast Hill Lane. At a bend bear R uphill on an enclosed footpath. Turn L on a lane. A young green woodpecker evaded a sparrow hawk here by flying about a yard over my head. The hawk's talons were clearly no match for my pointing finger and she turned back into the trees. At a fork go L down to houses and cross a stile between Vale Farm and Vale House. Fork R before a stile and perhaps enjoy the birdsong, including linnets, around the gorse to the L. Just past the second pond bear R uphill to the church gate. (If you have said your prayers already you can go straight on – see map.) There are fine views from the churchyard and you exit through the gate and down the lane back to the pub.

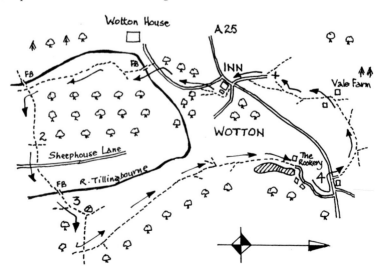